THE BATTLE OF MATAPAN

THE BATTLE
OF
MATAPAN

S. W. C. PACK

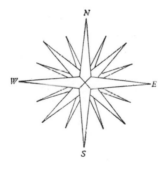

THE MACMILLAN COMPANY
NEW YORK

By the same author

WEATHER FORECASTING

ANSON'S VOYAGE (Abridged)

ADMIRAL LORD ANSON

etc.

First published in the United States of America, 1961

MADE AND PRINTED IN GREAT BRITAIN BY
WILLIAM CLOWES AND SONS LTD, LONDON AND BECCLES

For
Edie and Billie Belknap

PREFACE

THE battle of Matapan was fought on the 28th and 29th March, 1941, between the British and Italian Fleets, in the seas to the south and west of the island of Crete in the Mediterranean Sea, the main action taking place during the night of the 28th March about 100 miles off Cape Matapan in Greece.

At this time Britain stood virtually alone. Germany had overrun the Low Countries and Norway in the Spring of 1940. This had been followed, in June 1940, by the entry of Italy on the side of Germany and by the fall of France.

The battle is important from an historical point of view in a number of respects. It was the first time that carrier-borne aircraft played a vital and indispensable role in a main fleet action. It was also the first big action in which radar-equipped ships, acting as eyes in the night, tracked down an unsuspecting enemy. It was the first main fleet action since the battle of Jutland in 1916, and the first in the Mediterranean since the battle of the Nile in 1798. It was possibly the last occasion in history when a battlefleet at night sighted the immediate target by human eye; for, although the stopped *Pola* had been picked up by *Valiant*'s radar, it was some time after this that Cattaneo's cruisers and destroyers were suddenly sighted by eye, appearing through the darkness on a bearing entirely different from that of the stopped *Pola*.

The Italian Fleet under Admiral Iachino was distinctly superior in speed and could, theoretically, manœuvre so as to choose the most favourable range, or could decline action at will. The new *Vittorio Veneto* class of battleship had a speed of over 30 knots and was equipped with a powerful armament of nine 15-inch guns capable of firing with

7

accuracy at a range of 16 miles, and a secondary armament of twelve 6-inch guns. Iachino was also greatly superior in cruisers, six of which were large 10,000-ton ships heavily armoured against 6-inch fire, and equipped with 8-inch guns that could easily outrange the four British 6-inch gun cruisers.

The British Fleet under Admiral Cunningham was, in the main, old and slow. Nevertheless his fleet was high in operational efficiency and morale, and was manned by officers and men who were proud of a great tradition. Cunningham, aware of his material inferiority, and the challenge to Britain's control of the Mediterranean, had missed no opportunity to bring about a decisive fleet action, so as to reduce, if possible, Italy's superiority. His policy had always been to take the bold and direct course, but the Italians, with their newer and faster ships, had so far eluded him.

In one respect, and one only, Cunningham was at a great material advantage, and that was in the possession of an armoured aircraft carrier, the *Formidable*. Between the First and Second World Wars acrid discussion had gone on for many years. The antagonists pointed out that the carrier was no match for either cruiser or battleship, and would be a perpetual liability in a fleet, needing the protection of the big guns of a battlefleet besides its own heavy armour, and also a screen of anti-submarine destroyers. The Italians had decided against carriers. The protagonists, on the other hand, pointed out that here was a new long-range weapon. A carrier's aircraft could achieve a vast and effective reconnaissance, compared with which a search by a cruiser would be as ineffectual as looking for a needle in a haystack. The carrier's aircraft could also strike with bombs or torpedoes at a range of 100 miles or more, and could provide fighter protection against shore-based bombers for the whole fleet. The British had decided for carriers, and *Formidable* was one of the products. She entered the Mediterranean only a few

8

days before the battle of Matapan. Her part in the battle is described in this book. Without her there would have been no main action because of the Italian superiority of speed. In her absence the results of the skirmishes off Gavdo on the morning of the 28th March might have been highly adverse to the British ships. In his despatch Admiral Cunningham paid particular tribute to the magnificent work of the Fleet Air Arm.

Strategically, the results of the battle, in which the Italians lost three heavy cruisers and two destroyers, brought about a substantial reduction in the material superiority of the Italian Fleet. The heavy cruisers had been a constant menace not only to the lighter armed and slower British cruisers but to all British light ships. But the battle had an even greater result which was most important for subsequent operations, and particularly in the evacuation of the British army from Greece and Crete. The Italian Fleet, had it wished, could have obstructed and upset this difficult work; but it did not appear, nor did it again voluntarily offer action. This fact can be directly attributed to the severe treatment received at the battle of Matapan.

I am most grateful to Admiral of the Fleet Viscount Cunningham of Hyndhope, K.T., G.C.B., O.M., D.S.O., LL.D., who read my original typescript, and referred to it as "a very accurate and interesting account". My thanks are also due to those many friends and old shipmates who have given their assistance or provided first-hand descriptions of the various phases, thus bringing verisimilitude to an account of a battle which was amazingly full of errors, coincidences, and surprises. Although I have not been able to quote from all contributions, they have all proved helpful, particularly in describing events which have been forgotten in the course of nineteen years or which at the time were obscure or not understood.

I am indebted to My Lords Commissioners of the Admiralty for access to Admiralty records and for permission to publish. I am also grateful for help so readily given by the Keeper of Photographs at the Imperial War Museum, and by the Admiralty Librarian and the staff of the Admiralty Historical Section.

I am indebted to authors and publishers for permission to quote extracts from the following:

> *Gavdo e Matapan*, by Admiral A. Iachino
> *A Sailor's Odyssey*, by Viscount Cunningham (Hutchinson)
> *Before The Tide Turned*, by Hugh Hodgkinson (Harrap)

Finally, my deepest thanks are due to my hosts at Ilaro Court where most of the text was written. To them I dedicate this book with affection and gratitude.

Ilaro Court   S. W. C. P.
Barbados
March 1960

CONTENTS

CONTENTS

LIST OF ILLUSTRATIONS

THE DIAGRAMS

ACKNOWLEDGMENT

THE Author and Publishers wish to thank the following for permission to reproduce the illustrations appearing in this book:

G. A. Balshaw and the Canberra Australian War Memorial, for figs. 9 and 10.
Admiral of the Fleet Viscount Cunningham of Hyndhope, K.T., G.C.B., O.M., D.S.O., LL.D., for fig. 6.
Admiral Iachino, for figs. 7, 11, 12, and 20–4.
The Imperial War Museum, for figs. 1–5, 8, 13–15, 25–30, 32, and 33.
The Navy Office, Canberra, for fig. 31.
The Times, for figs. 16–19.

The Publishers have been unable to trace the source of the photographs which appear as figs. 34–6, and would be grateful for information regarding them so that proper acknowledgment may be made in future editions of this book.

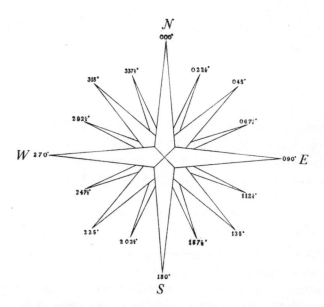

All courses and bearings have been referred to in the three-figure system where 000° to 360° covers the whole range of compass courses, e.g. 045° = North-east.

For simplicity all times in the text have been given in the 12-hour system, a.m. or p.m., except in quoted signals and the diagrams where the official 24-hour system has been retained.

I

The Bait

"Subject: Naval Strategic Situation in the Mediterranean.
From: German Naval Liaison Officer, Rome.
To: Italian Naval Staff.
Date: 19th March 1941.

"The German Naval Staff considers that at the moment there is only one British battleship, *Valiant*, in the Eastern Mediterranean fully ready for action. It is not anticipated that heavy British units will be withdrawn from the Atlantic in the near future. Force H is also considered unlikely to appear in the Mediterranean.

"Thus the situation in the Mediterranean is at the moment more favourable for the Italian Fleet than ever before. Intensive traffic from Alexandria to the Greek ports, whereby the Greek forces are receiving constant reinforcements in men and equipment, presents a particularly worthwhile target for the Italian Naval forces.

"The German Naval Staff considers that the appearance of Italian units in the area south of Crete will seriously interfere with British shipping, and may even lead to the complete interruption of the transport of troops, especially as these transports are at the moment inadequately protected."

2

News of Italian Fleet Movements

Formidable was lying at her usual berth in Alexandria Harbour. Some time after noon on Thursday, 27th March 1941, there came the bustle of preparation for leaving harbour. This was unexpected as *Formidable* had returned to Alexandria only three days earlier, following a sweep with the Fleet to the north-west to cover operation LUSTRE: the convoying of British troops from Egypt to Greece. There was, however, no mistaking the fact that we were off again. Aircraft stores and ground crews were arriving, we could see the heavy arrester wires being rigged across the flight deck and hear the thrash of the crash-barriers undergoing test.

At 3.30 p.m. *Formidable* sailed, and about an hour later we turned into wind to fly on the squadrons from Dekheila airfield. This was always an inspiring sight. It was a lovely spring afternoon, typical of the Eastern Mediterranean at this time of year. The sky was almost a clear blue, except for a little tell-tale cirrus here and there, and the wind was light. We were faced with few meteorological worries and no immediate flying difficulties. We were proud of our ship *Formidable*, a brand-new armoured aircraft carrier of 23,000 tons and 31 knots. She had been commissioned four months earlier at Belfast, and had sailed all the way round by the Cape of Good Hope in order to enter the Eastern Mediterranean to relieve the damaged *Illustrious*. Entry through the Suez Canal had, however, been delayed several days owing to the presence of enemy mines, and we had not arrived at Alexandria until the 10th March. We had been busy ever since.

Formidable with her squadrons of fighters and torpedo bombers represented an indispensable contribution to the Fleet, adding not only the benefits of a long-range armament and a wide reconnaissance, but also vital defence from enemy shadowers and bombers. This was one sphere in which the British Mediterranean Fleet, under Admiral Sir Andrew Cunningham, K.C.B., D.S.O., had a distinct superiority over the Italian Fleet. In every other material factor, it was, on paper at any rate, inferior. Ships were older and slower, and guns were smaller; and in the matter of destroyers, Cunningham was desperately short. Britain was fortunate in that a decision had been taken in the late 'thirties, albeit in spite of severe opposition, to build armoured carriers and to proceed with the development of the Fleet Air Arm. Italy had decided against carriers, Mussolini adopting the argument that nowhere in the Mediterranean could his fleet be far from the protection which could be provided by shore-based aircraft.

Our squadrons had been with *Formidable* long enough for us to know the air crews well by now, and this added to the interest of the air arrival. There were those who always made a perfect landing. There were also those who nearly always just slithered on or dropped from a height at the frantic bidding of Lieutenant-Commander Simon Borrett, the bat-man, and continued bouncing until their hook caught a late arrester wire or they fetched up in the crash-barrier.

Captain Mike Haworth, D.S.C., R.N., then a lieutenant observer, writes:

> "I was serving in an Albacore Squadron belonging to *Formidable*, which was disembarked at the Naval Air Station at Dekheila, about three miles outside Alexandria, when about noon on the 27th we received the order for a rush embarkation. This is an Air Squadron's equivalent to raising steam and involved several hundred men in several hours' labour which would make a pre-war Monday forenoon's general drill look like the reading room of the Athenaeum by comparison. We thought at first that we were going to sea for exercises, and even when, that evening, crews were briefed for a dawn search, no general inkling of what was afoot was let out."

Full of interest we watched the squadrons land on, wondering what our destination or objective was to be this time. Later in the day our conjectures increased when we learnt that the battlefleet also had left Alexandria after dark. Soon we were steaming together at 20 knots to the north-westward, the three 15-inch battleships, *Warspite*, *Barham*, and *Valiant*, the armoured aircraft carrier *Formidable*, and an anti-submarine screen of nine destroyers, *Jervis*, *Janus*, *Nubian*, *Mohawk*, *Stuart*, *Greyhound*, *Griffin*, *Hotspur*, and *Havock*.* All ships were darkened. The Commander-in-Chief, Admiral Cunningham, was in *Warspite*.

Excitement grew as we learnt that the Italian Fleet had been reported at sea, presumably looking for a rich plum in the shape of a British troop convoy. There had been no major fleet action since the Battle of Jutland in 1916, and it was generally felt that one might be brewing now. The first lieutenant of the *Formidable*, Lieutenant-Commander George Codrington-Ball, remarked that all three of our battleships had fought at Jutland, twenty-five years earlier, and were very old in comparison with the new Italian battleships such as *Vittorio Veneto* and *Littorio*.

Operation LUSTRE had begun on the 4th March, most of the troops embarking in H.M. ships, their equipment and stores being carried in merchant ships provided with light escort. To cover these movements, Vice-Admiral, Light Forces, Vice-Admiral H. D. Pridham-Wippell, with four cruisers *Orion*, *Ajax*, *Perth*, and *Gloucester*, and four destroyers *Ilex*, *Hasty*, *Hereward*, and *Vendetta*, was at present operating in the Aegean Sea.

On receipt of a report from a British flying boat at 12.20 p.m. on the 27th March, that a force of three Italian cruisers and a destroyer had been sighted eighty miles east of the south-eastern tip of Sicily, proceeding to the south-eastward, roughly in the direction of Crete, Admiral Cunningham had assumed the possibility of Italian battleships being at sea in support. If this were true he was anxious not to appear to be aware of their movements. It was fortunate that there was only one British convoy at sea, A.G.9, at that moment, and it was to the southward of Crete, bound for the Piraeus with troops. Cunningham directed that it

* See Appendix I.

1 *The flight deck officer signals with the bats to an Albacore about to land*

2 *A Fulmar comes in to land*

3　*An Albacore taking off, while others in the background await their turn*
(H.M.S. "Formidable")

4　*An Albacore taking off from H.M.S. "Formidable"*

should continue until dark, and then reverse course. The sailing of a south-bound convoy from the Piraeus was cancelled. He also decided to keep the British battleships in harbour until night-fall. An Italian reconnaissance aircraft from Rhodes flew over Alexandria at 2 p.m. that afternoon and reported seeing three battleships, two aircraft carriers, and an uncertain number of cruisers in harbour. Evidently the British were suspecting nothing. Since the 25th March there had been a noticeable increase in Italian efforts to watch the movements of the British Mediterranean Fleet and to obtain a frequent reconnaissance of Alexandria harbour, and this had led Cunningham to believe that an Italian Fleet operation was imminent. The most likely operation would be an attack on the lightly escorted British convoys, but it was pretty certain that such an operation would not take place if it were known that the British Fleet had left harbour. Another possibility was an Italian Fleet diversion to cover a landing in Greece or Cyrenaica, or an attack on Malta.

Certain precautionary measures had been taken on the 26th March and were immediately amended as necessary after receipt of the report of sighting Italian cruisers and destroyers on the afternoon of the 27th March. Pridham-Wippell with his force of cruisers and destroyers was now ordered to be in a position thirty miles south of Gavdo Island—a rocky islet twenty miles south of Crete—at 6.30 a.m. the next morning, 28th March. The Royal Air Force, who had been asked to stand by with thirty Blenheim bombers of Nos. 84, 113, and 211 Squadrons in Greece, were now requested to provide air reconnaissance over the south Ionian Sea, the south-west Aegean, and over the sea to the south of Crete. A Greek destroyer force had already been warned to be at short notice.

Cunningham, in *A Sailor's Odyssey*, refers to his own private cover plan, which involved going ashore during the afternoon with an obvious suitcase, to make it appear that he would be spending the night ashore. He returned to *Warspite* immediately after dark; the Fleet sailed at 7.0 p.m. Captain T. M. Brownrigg, C.B.E., D.S.O., R.N. who was then master of the Fleet says:

"This operation was planned in the morning and we intentionally sent principal staff officers away by air during the day so as to allay all the Italian agents' apprehension; we also kept our awnings spread and the Admiral invited people to dinner. As soon as it was dark we furled our awnings, the officers returned and the dinner was cancelled."

We did not know at the time that the Italian Naval Staff had been informed by the German Naval Liaison Officer in Rome that only one British battleship, the *Valiant*, was fully ready for action, the *Warspite* and *Barham* having been damaged in bombing attacks in Alexandria. Nor did we know that the Italians had been told that the intensive traffic from Alexandria to Greece presented a particularly worthwhile target and was inadequately protected.

Excitement was high throughout the Fleet as we sped to the north-westward on this lovely night, and, although we knew little as yet of either the composition of the Italian forces or their exact intentions, there was a confident feeling that we were on the eve of a major action which would at last give us the opportunity of improving the balance of sea power in the Mediterranean in our favour, an opportunity which Cunningham had been trying to bring about ever since Italy had entered the war on the 10th June 1940.

Watchkeepers excepted, most of us turned in soon to prepare for an early start the next day, wondering very much what the day would bring, and with the thought that this might be the last night that many of us would enjoy. Perhaps there were similar thoughts in the opposing fleet whose presence at sea was as yet no more than hypothetical.

3

The Balance of Power in the Eastern Mediterranean

TO UNDERSTAND the implications of the battle of Cape Matapan one should know the background of events which had taken place after the entry of Italy into the war on 10th June 1940. At that time our position in the Mediterranean looked desperate. The Italian Navy was vastly superior to the British Mediterranean Fleet in numbers, and her ships were generally newer, faster, and better armed. Moreover with the fall of France the attitude of the French Fleet was uncertain.

By firm persuasion and supreme tact throughout a period of painful and difficult negotiations, Cunningham, with the aid of his staff and the captains of H.M. ships in the Fleet, had been able to arrange for the neutralisation and immobilisation of the French warships under Vice-Admiral Godfroy at Alexandria, so that there was no danger of their falling into enemy hands.

The British Mediterranean Fleet had been strengthened and its main base shifted eastwards from Malta to Alexandria, but this had only been possible by denuding forces in home waters. As the possibility of invasion of the United Kingdom still remained, the accession of strength in the Mediterranean had to be severely limited. The Western Mediterranean was covered by Force H under Vice-Admiral Sir James Somerville.

There had been a number of fleet skirmishes with the Italians but no full-scale action. Cunningham was keen to attack the Italian Fleet as soon as possible, but his main concern was Malta, which many now thought untenable. Malta was close to the no-man's-land of the Sicilian Narrows which connected the western and eastern ends of the Mediterranean but which was dominated by enemy bombers. The possession of Malta with adequate fighter protection could neutralise such air domination, but it meant that Malta itself would be an obvious target for heavy and determined attacks by the enemy. The Navy had for almost a century and a half regarded Malta as the principal base on which the command of the Mediterranean Sea depended. Within a few weeks of Italy's entry into the war, Malta began to run short of provisions. Much of the food supply for the vast civil population had in peacetime arrived in small trading vessels from Sicily and Italy, but no practical alternative had been arranged in the event of Italy entering the war. It was fortunate for Malta that the Italians had made no preparation for an all-out assault during their nine months of neutrality. Instead, a slow siege began, and Malta was daily and nightly subjected to heavy bombing from the air.

Cunningham was determined to gain command of the sea and to keep it. Convoys were run to Malta with troops and provisions from Alexandria, and convoys in reverse carried to Alexandria much needed equipment and technical services which were becoming necessary for the repair and maintenance of the Fleet in this relatively ill-equipped base. The Commander-in-Chief also regarded these convoys as providing tempting opportunities for the Italian Fleet to put to sea, for all ship movements were known through their excellent air reconnaissance, and this he felt might lead to a trial of strength. This in fact happened off Calabria in July 1940 when it appeared that a fleet action was imminent against two Italian battleships, twelve cruisers, and a large number of destroyers. The Italian Fleet flagship was hit by the *Warspite*'s accurate firing at a range of 13 miles, and the action was immediately broken off, the only casualty being an Italian destroyer.

Cunningham's aggressive leadership was, however, not enough to redress the material balance of Italian superiority, and he had informed the First Sea Lord that he must have at least one other battleship, additional to the modernised *Warspite*, that could fire at a range comparable with the two new Italian 35,000-ton, 15-inch battleships *Littorio* and *Vittorio Veneto*. He further stressed the vital need for one of the new armoured aircraft carriers and the need for fighter protection for the Fleet and convoys when close to the enemy shore. As a result, the modernised old battleship *Valiant*, sister ship of the *Warspite*, and the new armoured aircraft carrier *Illustrious*, together with two newly converted anti-aircraft cruisers *Calcutta* and *Coventry*, sailed from the westward through the Mediterranean, escorted by Force H under Somerville, and after passing unescorted through the Sicilian Narrows at night, joined the Mediterranean Fleet between Malta and Pantellaria after the Fleet had escorted a convoy of three merchant ships and a tanker from Alexandria to Malta. Cunningham speaks in glowing terms of this accretion of strength. Both *Valiant* and *Illustrious* were fitted with radar and could therefore give warning of attacking aircraft forty or fifty miles away. But the greatest relief was in the possession of the fighters in the carrier, which could minimise the effect of enemy bomber attacks and allow the Fleet considerably more freedom of movement and planning. These additions did much to reduce the material superiority enjoyed by the Italians.

The difference had been further reduced on the night of 11th November 1940, when *Illustrious* approached to within 170 miles of Taranto and flew off naval aircraft to attack the Italian Fleet lying in harbour. One battleship, the *Cavour*, was sunk by torpedo, and two others, the new *Littorio* and the older *Duilio*, were damaged and put out of action. A cruiser and destroyer together with certain port installations were hit by bombs. This raid also had the effect of weakening Italian morale considerably, and of forcing the Italians to withdraw many of their ships to more remote ports, a big factor when attempting to pass convoys through the Mediterranean. It was a tremendous encouragement for British morale at a time when the general scene looked dark but in particular it was a great distinction for the Fleet Air Arm with its gallant band of young pilots, observers, and gunners, many of whom, though as yet relatively inexperienced, had at last come into their own with a magnificent success.

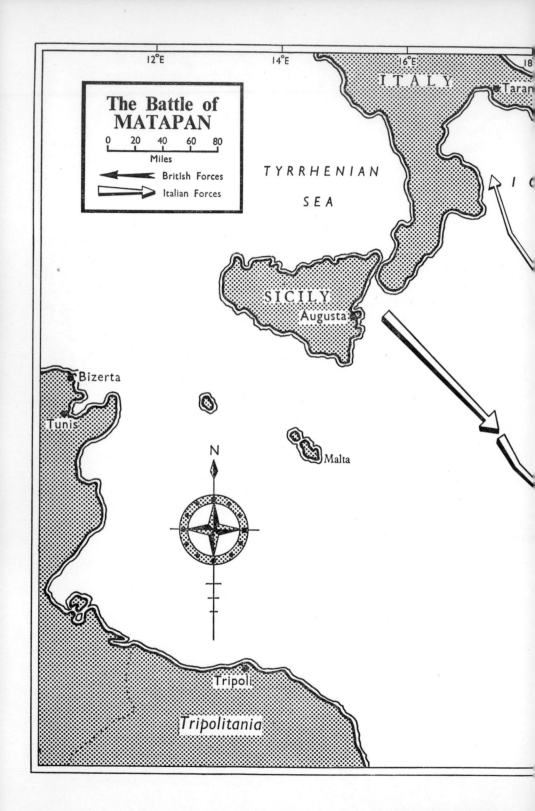

The Battle of
MATAPAN

0   20   40   60   80
Miles

British Forces
Italian Forces

TYRRHENIAN

SEA

ITALY

Taran

IO

SICILY

Augusta

Bizerta

Tunis

Malta

N

Tripoli

Tripolitania

12°E   14°E   16°E   18

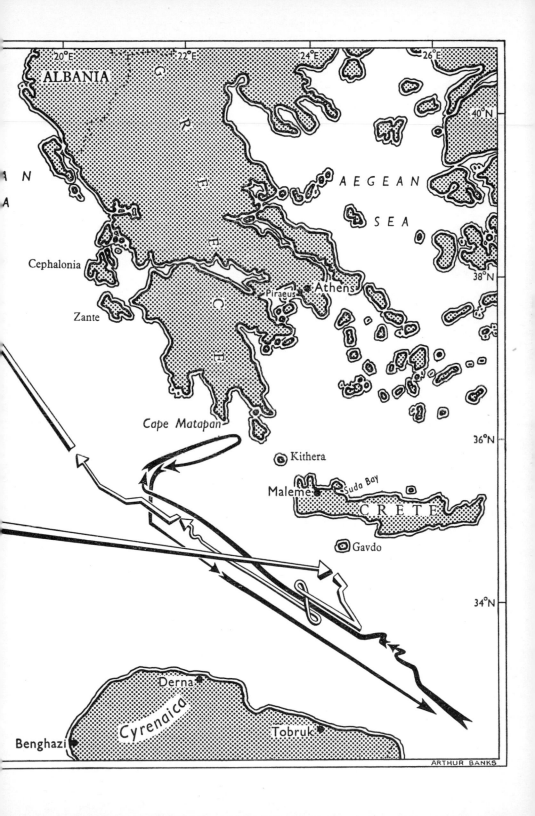

Hitler had tried to woo Franco in October 1940 at Hendaye, but Franco had refused to allow him to send an army group through Spain to Gibraltar, Algeria, and Tunisia, in an attempt to seal off the Mediterranean from British domination. Hitler thereupon turned his attacks to a German thrust through the Balkans with the idea of neutralising Turkey and Greece and threatening the British positions in the Eastern Mediterranean. Detailed planning began in November 1940. Hitler also sent his well-trained Fliegerkorps X to stiffen the Italian Regia Aeronautica in Sicily. This was to have a profound effect later in increasing the local air superiority enjoyed by the enemy over the narrow waters between Sicily and Tunisia. To the dangers of high level bombing was now added accurate and deadly dive bombing by Stukas.

Meanwhile the apparent improvement of the British position in the Mediterranean received a tremendous boost when General Wavell began his offensive in the Western Desert in early December 1940, his forces under General O'Connor advancing five hundred miles in the next two months, encircling Italian strongholds one after another on the African Coast, and capturing 130,000 Italian prisoners, 400 tanks, and 850 guns. This penetration continued as far as Benghazi, coastal support being provided in the shape of bombardment and supply by ships of the Inshore Squadron. In early January 1941 the moment was seized to pass a convoy of four merchant ships through the Mediterranean from the west, three of them with urgent supplies for our Greek allies, and the fourth with a vital cargo for Malta. The convoy was met by the battleships *Warspite* and *Valiant* and the carrier *Illustrious* in the narrows to the north-west of Malta, and shortly afterwards *Illustrious* in particular was subjected to heavily concentrated attacks by dive bombers of the Luftwaffe. Badly damaged and on fire, she limped into Malta where she was again bombed. After a few days she succeeded in returning to Alexandria but she could no longer operate aircraft. The Fleet was once more without the services of an armoured carrier. It was then that *Formidable* was diverted from the Atlantic, to round Africa, and enter the Mediterranean through the Suez Canal to relieve *Illustrious*.

To make matters worse, Rommel arrived at Tripoli in February 1941 with German armour, preparing for the lightning strike which would recover all the ground lost by the Italians, and take him to the gates of Egypt.

The convoys continued: the Germans and Italians working southwards from Sicily to sustain the African offensive; the British working east and west to provide for Malta, and northwards from Egypt to lend support to the sorely threatened Greeks, now faced with a severer foe than that which had attacked them when Mussolini had struck at them in late October 1940.

With the entry of *Formidable* into the Mediterranean, accompanied by 803 Fighter Squadron of Fulmars, and 826 and 829 Torpedo Reconnaissance Squadrons of Albacores, Cunningham received his much needed replacement for *Illustrious*. After the short passage from Port Said to Alexandria *Formidable* came through the Great Pass and entered harbour at 10.30 a.m. on Monday, the 10th March. In the harbour were *Warspite*, *Valiant*, and *Barham*, the submarine parent-ship *Medway*, the damaged *Illustrious*, the old aircraft carrier *Eagle*, long overdue for a refit, and many ships of varied size and class, including the immobilised French warships. We passed *Warspite*, and saluted the flag of the Commander-in-Chief. We were given a welcoming cheer from *Illustrious*. We felt rather like the new batsman walking to the wicket, and we could imagine the remarks: "I wonder how long she'll last." "I give 'em six weeks at the most." But it was now that we realised the excitement of being once again with the Fleet. The next morning *Formidable* hoisted the flag of Acting Rear-Admiral Denis Boyd, promoted Rear-Admiral Mediterranean Aircraft Carriers from the *Illustrious* which he had brought safely back to Alexandria from "bomb alley". Seventeen days later we were steaming at 20 knots with the battlefleet in the direction of Cape Matapan.

4

British Viewpoint

THE VICTOR at Matapan, now Admiral of the Fleet Viscount Cunningham of Hyndhope, K.T., G.C.B., O.M., D.S.O., was known throughout the Navy as ABC, an abbreviation for Andrew Brown Cunningham. It is appropriate to say a word about this great seaman and leader and the feeling in the Fleet at this time. Admiration and affection for the Commander-in-Chief were universal, and his burning desire to get to grips with the enemy was shared by all. There was so much to be done in the increasing requirements to escort convoys and transport troops, in addition to aggressive forays at every opportunity, that life in the Fleet was particularly strenuous, especially so in destroyers. The main tactical purpose of destroyers is to attack and destroy enemy ships, but they were now being used as maids-of-all-work with multifarious duties such as anti-submarine screening, anti-aircraft fire, aircraft-carrier attendants, escorts, and carriers of troops, stores, and equipment. Much of this work had to be done in areas which were now becoming increasingly dominated by the Luftwaffe so that determined and accurate dive bombing was now added to the dangers of high level bombing. All this required long hours at action stations. One destroyer captain has said that "1940 and 1941 covered probably the hardest fighting of the war". Nevertheless in spite of lack of sleep and shortage of ships, the spirit in the Fleet was cock-a-hoop and there was always the feeling that a showdown with the Italian Fleet could not long be delayed, and that ABC would somehow or other arrange it.

Nowadays a naval Commander-in-Chief has his headquarters

ashore, but at the time of Matapan Cunningham had his headquarters in *Warspite*, and was attended by a chief of staff and an
operational staff of officers, mainly of commander's rank, consisting of the staff operations officer, fleet gunnery officer, fleet
torpedo officer, fleet navigation officer (master of the fleet), and
the fleet signal officer: a staff, in the words of the fleet gunnery
officer, "microscopic compared to the serried ranks of brigadiers
in Cairo and the large staffs which collected later in the war for
Allied Force Headquarters". ABC was not one to suffer fools
gladly and it is obvious that he would require every one of his
staff to be on the top line and ready with an expert and speedy
answer to any queries concerning a particular specialisation. He
himself had spent a large part of his service life in destroyers and
presumably had the "salt horse" attitude towards many of the
specialisations. It is interesting to read some comments of the
fleet gunnery officer, now Vice-Admiral Sir Geoffrey Barnard,
K.C.B., D.S.O., who had the "privilege of being within earshot
of his Commander-in-Chief" on many occasions, and in particular
at Matapan.

> "ABC had a healthy respect for the gun as a weapon *if
> properly used*," says Barnard, "and an almost boyish delight in
> the sound of guns going off in a good cause; but he must have
> suffered much from earnest gunnery officers in the course of his
> Service career. As a result anything savouring of long-range gun
> actions with 'black magic' about curvature of the earth, and
> canted trunnions and all that, was anathema to him. He had
> been confirmed in this view early in the war when, in a long-
> range chase of Italian destroyers by four British cruisers, each
> one commanded by a gallant and distinguished gunnery officer,
> the entire reserve of 6-inch ammunition in the Eastern
> Mediterranean had been expended in an hour, with serious
> repercussions on subsequent operations. His views on
> gunnery were more often given verbally than on paper."

Barnard then refers to the long-winded technical reports
entitled "Progress in Naval Gunnery" which it was customary to
send in annually in pre-war days, but which for lack of time during
the stress of planning and operational work had been neglected
in 1940 and 1941. In response to a hastener from the Admiralty,

ABC, with tongue in cheek, gave verbal directions for a report to be written in the following sense:

> "There has been NO progress in gunnery in the Mediterranean in the years 1940 and 1941, but certain old lessons well known to Noah and the Armada have been re-learned at much trouble and expense. The most notable lesson is that the right range for any ship of the Mediterranean Fleet, from a battleship to a submarine, to engage an enemy ship with gunfire is POINT BLANK (nowadays 2,000 yards or less) AT WHICH RANGE EVEN A GUNNERY OFFICER CANNOT MISS."

"To understand this," says Barnard, "is to understand a lot about Matapan."

It also helps us to understand a lot about Cunningham. He was a great believer in being up to date, but any embellishment had to be seen to work and have a useful life. Correspondingly he was a great stickler for discipline and the customs of the Service embodying correct dress and ceremony, but he would waive such matters when it was in the interest of the Service to do so. He always had the common-sense outlook and practical attitude of "let's get on with it" and this endeared him to officers and ratings alike. An incident which occurred at Alexandria is worth telling. A motor boat belonging to an Australian destroyer was leaving the shore jetty when a man in plain clothes asked the coxswain if he could put him on board *Warspite* as he passed. The coxswain agreed, but he told the man, whom he believed to be the *Warspite*'s canteen manager, that he would have to jump for the ladder as they passed *Warspite*'s gangway, owing to clutch trouble which prevented the boat from going astern. The passenger duly jumped as the boat swept past the flagship's middle gangway. On arrival at his own ship the coxswain was shown a signal from the Commander-in-Chief to the commanding officer thanking him for the lift, and only then realised the identity of the passenger whom he had peremptorily addressed.

Because the Fleet was so often at sea it was usually in a poor state of maintenance and refit and this was a handicap to speed and operational, efficiency. Such a condition however, was more than compensated by the high morale and keenness which goes with

5 *Admiral Sir Andrew Cunningham, Commander-in-Chief, Mediterranean Fleet, comes on board flotilla leader to congratulate the captains of destroyers*

6 *Admiral Sir Andrew Cunningham on admiral's bridge of H.M.S. "Warspite" at Matapan on the morning of 28th March 1941*

7 "Zara", "Pola", "Fiume," and "Garibaldi" seen from "Abruzzi". The 1st and 8th cruiser divisions of the Italian fleet early on the morning of the Battle of Matapan

intense activity, and the frequent occasions when guns had to be fired ensured that the gear worked and that crews were experienced. There was never any opportunity, however, for exercising night-action stations with the battlefleet, a practice which had been regularly and efficiently carried out in the years between the two World Wars. There were many young officers and ratings who had little idea of the intricacies of a night action and the accepted rules for searchlight procedure, starshell illumination, and the arrangements for rapid shift of target. Only those who had experienced such exercises in peacetime could realise the necessity for precise rules and the need for practice of swift manœuvre in the dark, to prepare for a possible action which might be all over in a matter of a few minutes. At this time, the night was regarded not as a time for action, but as a period of relative relaxation for ships which had been hard pressed by bombers during daylight hours.

But the main mood in the Fleet at this time was a reflection of Cunningham's determination to get to grips with the enemy. Barnard writes:

> "Whenever enemy forces were reported at sea in a position which gave us a possible chance of interception before they could get back home, ABC's burning desire to get at them and utterly destroy them would at once become evident to those of the staff who knew the form. He would pace one side of the Admiral's bridge, always the side nearest the enemy; the speed of advance of the battleship was never fast enough for him and every second was grudged when a turn from the main line of advance was required for operating aircraft. This mood was known colloquially among the staff as the 'caged tiger act' and we adjusted our actions accordingly; there were many times and places when ABC would allow his junior staff officers to 'speak out of turn', but these occasions were not one of them. It was always, for all beholders, an inspiring example of single-minded concentration on the one object of getting to close grips with the enemy.
>
> "On this occasion (Matapan), the speed of advance of the battlefleet was not bad, in spite of the *Warspite* having slight condenseritis and the *Barham*, as usual, having to cut corners on the zig-zag, or when the *Formidable* was operating aircraft. On the whole, we were getting on better than in the early days of the war, when the *Malaya* and *Royal*

Sovereign were the retarding influences on the speed of the battlefleet. At intervals a smile could be seen on the face of the tiger."

On this occasion the normal stimulation of proceeding to sea had been augmented by the receipt of reconnaissance reports from an R.A.F. flying boat. Enemy cruisers were at sea and steering east. And where there were cruisers there might with some luck be also battleships in support. Perhaps the time had come.

"ABC was on the top of his form," says Barnard, "and pulled the legs of the staff officers on duty." A quiet night was spent in cruising watches, since there was no prospect of surface contact before dawn.

5

Dawn Search

ABLE SEAMAN RESTALL, my meteorological assistant, called me at
4.15 a.m. the next morning, the 28th, with the usual "Balloon's
ready, Sir", and added "Not a bad morning, neither." It was pitch
dark and the sky was overcast, but there was no rain. There had
been no further news about the Italians, but there was plenty of
time yet. *Formidable* was steaming north-westward at 20 knots in
company with the battlefleet and destroyers. At dawn we were to
close up at action stations and fly off a search force to look for the
enemy. Here were the modern eyes of the fleet, never used before
in a major fleet action, that could search an area hundreds of miles
away, and report speedily back to the Commander-in-Chief. Before
take-off, however, they must be furnished with information about
weather, visibility, cloud, and, in particular, wind speed and direction at certain heights. Such information, vital though it was in
both planning and execution, could not easily be obtained. The
area of interest was an extensive one: a vast sea, from which little
or no weather information was obtainable, surrounded by land
from which routine weather reports, if they existed, were secret.
Nevertheless an organisation had been developed whereby a
collection of synoptic weather reports could be received at routine
times in the carrier, which after being deciphered and plotted
could provide a sketchy weather map of the region; a somewhat out-
of-date map, with many blanks more especially in the areas towards
enemy territory, but one which, when studied by an expert in
conjunction with the carrier's own recorded observations of wind
and weather, could provide a basis on which to plan an operation.

The winds at various levels were obtained by observing the direction and elevation, every minute, of a large balloon which prior to release had been filled with hydrogen and carefully balanced to ensure a known rate of ascent. This sounds easy, but on a pitch black night in a strong wind it required ingenuity and experience. On this particular morning everything went smoothly. Though the surface wind was fresh, about 24 knots, it was blowing from abaft the starboard beam, and we were able to get the balloon away without bursting or catching it in the superstructure. No visible lights were permitted on deck, so the balloon had to have an attachment which consisted of a small torch bulb screwed into a dry battery, totally enclosed by a light metal cloak which dropped off automatically at a suitable period after the balloon's release. In practice the snags were many. Either the balloon would burst before release, because of the high relative wind down the flight deck, or the metal cloak would fall off too soon after release, or refuse to fall off at all. On one occasion a balloon lodged in the lattice work of the top of a portable crane on the flight deck; and there it stayed. As the cloak dropped from the attached lamp, a beckoning light was exposed for any lurking submarine to see. A frantic climb up the crane followed, and the errant light was rescued after what seemed minutes, at a cost of no more than a badly barked shin.

Apart from look-outs there were few on deck on this particular Friday morning, for it was still two hours to dawn. Through the captain's sight on the island we followed the balloon until it disappeared in cloud after a little more than seven minutes. This indicated a cloud base of five thousand feet. Then followed the working out of the strength and direction of winds at various levels, and the plotting of a weather chart: all routine work when at sea, but on this particular morning one was very much aware that a momentous day was about to dawn and wind and weather would be important factors. If the Italian Fleet were really at sea, a trial of strength was imminent which would probably decide once and for all in whose hands should rest the control of shipping in the Mediterranean.

At 5.30 a.m. it was still dark as air crews came to the island to enter the briefing room. Aircraft were being ranged on the flight deck. The noise of their warming up was a welcome sound. There were indications that the weather would improve, cloud would lift, and the surface wind, now fresh from the north-east, would gradually back to a direction more suitable for flying on and off, while on our present course to the north-west.

For their air navigation the crews were principally concerned with upper winds, but the surface wind was also a vital factor inasmuch as *Formidable* must turn into wind each time aircraft were flown off or on, and hence delay the speed of advance of the Fleet. Independent action was not possible without disrupting or reducing the overall effective value of the anti-submarine screen provided by the destroyers, and supplemented during daylight hours by *Formidable's* aircraft.

As the battlefleet left harbour the night before, *Warspite* had passed too near a mud-bank which fouled her condensers and reduced her speed. The speed of the Fleet was therefore limited to 20 knots. This fact was to have important consequences.

By 5.55 a.m. our force had reached a position roughly 150 miles to the southward of the eastern end of Crete. There was just enough light to see across the flight deck. *Formidable* now turned into wind, and one by one the aircraft roared along the length of the flight deck and took off to form up the dawn search. As each passed the region of the bridge the pilot gave a thumbs up or similar sign. Excitement was now high. The grey dawn was slowly spreading from the east. Gradually the forms of the battleships came to view with the destroyers spread out in a screen beyond them. The sky assumed a golden hue. The clouds were slowly lifting and breaking. Visibility was about fifteen miles. Now began the long wait for first reports to come in.

About three-quarters of an hour after dawn we fell out from our stations. Watchkeepers, including certain look-outs and gunnery numbers, remained closed up. For the rest of us there was time for a brief respite. A quick bath, a shave, and a hurried help-yourself breakfast in the various messes from cereals, boiled eggs, and coffee or tea that had already been laid out.

An hour after the departure of the search force hopes began to fade. No sighting reports had come in. As further minutes passed, excitement waned. "Just another ruddy wild goose chase", muttered the first lieutenant. And one by one we began to feel that the report of the previous day must have been a false alarm. Or perhaps the Italian Fleet had returned to base after the brief sally. We had practically given up hope when the bugle sounded for action stations. Throughout the ship the call was broadcast on the amplifying system. Breakfasts were hurriedly abandoned. Steel helmets, respirators, and anti-flash clothing were donned. Fire parties, damage control groups, medical teams, and messing caterers closed up at speed. The steel ladders in the island rang with the clatter of boots as men doubled to their stations. And then the long wait began again. But this time it was a wait for what was expected to be exciting news.

My own job, in addition to providing current wind and weather information, was to keep a narrative of the battle, and my action station for this was on the compass platform.

The captain, A. W. La T. Bisset, conned his ship from this position, which was two decks up from the flight deck at the forward end of the island. Forward of the glass windows was a parapet from which the captain could gain an all-round view; particularly necessary for ship handling during dive bombing attacks. Opening off from the port side of the platform was a small projection overlooking the flight deck, and it was from here that "Skins" Atkinson, the Commander (Air), directed aircraft movements and flying generally.

One deck above was a smaller platform which was occupied by Rear-Admiral Dennis Boyd, D.S.C., Flag Officer, Mediterranean Aircraft Carriers.

The first report had arrived. At 7.20 a.m. our aircraft 5B signalled that she had sighted the enemy: this report placed four cruisers and four destroyers in 34° 22′ North, 24° 47′ East steering 230°, and was received in *Formidable* eight minutes later. This had been the reason why action stations had been sounded. Another signal followed from aircraft 5F, who reported that at 7.39 a.m. she had sighted four cruisers and six destroyers steering 220° in 34° 05' North, 24° 26' East.

These reports placed two enemy forces near Gavdo, steering roughly south-west, in positions well over a hundred miles to the north-west of us. Our aircraft had now been airborne for an hour and a half, and although reported aircraft positions were generally reliable, one had to accept the fact that accurate navigation could not be absolutely depended upon after such a passage of time. In addition to instrument errors and personal errors of observation and estimation, there would be errors due to variation of both wind speed and direction, not only at the various levels but also with the passage of time. Moreover, our initial estimation of the wind at a distance of 100 miles could in the absence of reliable reports be only conjectural. Again, although visibility was generally about fifteen miles, there were patches of mist which could lead to discrepancies in reports by different aircraft reporting the same force.

Although two separate enemy forces in positions twenty or so miles apart had therefore been reported, there was no certainty as yet that they were not one and the same force being reported by two different aircraft. Our doubts increased and disappointment grew when it became known that Pridham-Wippell had been ordered to rendezvous at 6.30 a.m. in a position to the south of Gavdo island. His force consisted of four cruisers and four destroyers, and conviction gradually spread that this must have been the subject of the two separate reports from aircraft 5B and 5F.

At 8.04 a.m. a further report was received from aircraft 5B amending his earlier enemy report of four cruisers and four destroyers to four cruisers and six destroyers. The report also stated that the enemy had altered course (from 230°) to 167°. There was hope now that this must refer to some force other than Pridham-Wippell's, for, whereas it might be possible to report a smaller number of vessels than were actually present, because of poor visibility, it was most improbable that a larger number would be reported.

Twenty minutes later, at 8.24 a.m., the situation took a dramatic turn when an emergency signal from *Orion* was intercepted. This reported three unknown vessels bearing north from her at a distance of eighteen miles, steering eastward. Excitement spread. There was now no doubt at all that the Italians were at sea. Their cruisers had been reported. It was probable that their battleships were also out in support, perhaps farther to the north-westward. Action was now almost certain. With present courses it would be possible to join action in less than two hours. The Commander-in-Chief ordered an increase of speed to 22 knots. This was *Warspite*'s maximum owing to her condenseritis. Anxiously we waited for further reports.

6

Cruiser Action off Gavdo

VICE-ADMIRAL PRIDHAM-WIPPELL had sailed in *Orion* from the Piraeus on Thursday, 27th March, with orders to be in position 34° 20′ North, 24° 10′ East with his cruisers and destroyers at 6.30 a.m. the next morning. The Commander-in-Chief in *Warspite* with the battlefleet and *Formidable* was at that time still 150 miles to the south-eastward, proceeding north-west at 20 knots.

Soon after reaching the rendezvous, Pridham-Wippell's force was sighted by an RO43, an Italian reconnaissance plane, which reported the composition of his force, four cruisers and four destroyers and also his course and speed, 135° at 18 knots. Pridham-Wippell thereupon ordered an alteration of course to 200° at 6.45 a.m., with the intention of turning away from the direction of probable reconnaissance, and proceeded at 20 knots.

On receipt of enemy reports from *Formidable*'s aircraft 5B and 5F which indicated two separate forces of Italian cruisers and destroyers within thirty miles of his own position, Pridham-Wippell assumed that it was his own force that had been reported by mistake. This opinion was also accepted by Cunningham in *Warspite* and Boyd in *Formidable*.

Pridham-Wippell's assumption was rudely shattered when at 7.45 a.m. one of *Orion*'s look-outs sighted smoke astern bearing 010°. A minute later it became clear that there was a force of enemy ships which was identified at 7.55 a.m. as three cruisers and three destroyers. This force consisted of the three Italian 10,000-ton cruisers *Trieste*, *Trento*, and *Bolzano* and the three 1,620-ton destroyers *Corazziere, Carabiniere,* and *Ascari.* Pridham-Wippell, correctly, believed the enemy cruisers to be armed with 8-inch guns which could outrange all four of his own 6-inch cruisers. He was also aware that, on paper at any rate, they were faster by $2\frac{1}{2}$ knots. He therefore determined to head straight for the Commander-in-Chief now 100 miles to the south-eastward, with the idea of leading this superior cruiser force towards the British battlefleet. Course was altered to 140°, and speed was increased to 28 knots. Shortly afterwards at 8.02 a.m. *Orion* made her enemy sighting report of three unknown vessels distant 18 miles on a bearing of 009°. These were the ships of the *Trieste* group and the rough position at 8.0 a.m. is shown in the diagram opposite. Though Pridham-Wippell was now fully aware of the *Trieste* group and had reported it as three unknown vessels, he was still unaware of the presence of yet another strong Italian force, quite close to him. This was the force whose position had been reported fairly accurately by *Formidable*'s aircraft 5B at 7.20 a.m., though discounted when it was assumed that the aircraft had mistakenly reported Pridham-Wippell's force. Aircraft 5B had amended his initial report of four cruisers and four destroyers to four cruisers and six destroyers at 7.46 a.m., but this signal was not received until after the *Trieste* group had been sighted by *Orion* and the exact position therefore remained obscure.

The presence of an additional strong force, of which Pridham-Wippell was quite unaware, placed him in an exceedingly vulnerable position, for it consisted of five cruisers and six destroyers situated in such a position that they could cut off Pridham-Wippell's withdrawal towards Cunningham. This force was made up of three 10,000-ton 8-inch cruisers *Zara, Fiume,* and *Pola,* two 8,000-ton 6-inch cruisers *Garibaldi* and *Abruzzi,* and the destroyers *Gioberti, Alfieri, Oriani, Carducci, Da Recco,* and *Pessagno.* There was still some doubt about the presence of the Italian battlefleet, though the feeling prevailed that it might be some miles astern of the cruisers. Aircraft 5F reported three Italian battleships at 8.05 a.m. in position 34° North 24° 16′ East, but this report was not received until almost an hour later, at

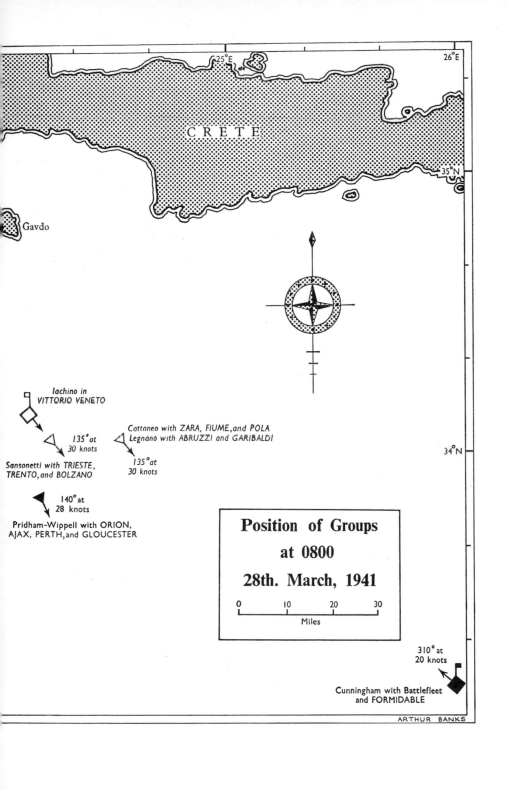

CRETE

Gavdo

Iachino in
VITTORIO VENETO

135° at
30 knots

Cattaneo with ZARA, FIUME, and POLA
Legnano with ABRUZZI and GARIBALDI

Sansonetti with TRIESTE,
TRENTO, and BOLZANO

135° at
30 knots

140° at
28 knots

Pridham-Wippell with ORION,
AJAX, PERTH, and GLOUCESTER

Position of Groups at 0800 28th. March, 1941

0	10	20	30
Miles

310° at
20 knots

Cunningham with Battlefleet
and FORMIDABLE

ARTHUR BANKS

which time it was regarded by Pridham-Wippell as "manifestly incorrect" since he himself had been only seven miles from the position at 8.05 a.m. and would have seen them.

At 8.12 a.m. Pridham-Wippell amplified his first sighting report and identified the force as three cruisers and an unknown number of destroyers, distant from him thirteen miles on a bearing of 010°. At this same moment the *Trieste* cruisers opened fire with their 8-inch guns. *Trieste* had sighted Pridham-Wippell's force at 7.58 a.m. and had reported them as being "Evidently bound for Alexandria". (See diagram p. 51.)

Opening salvoes from the Italians fell short of Pridham-Wippell's cruisers who, with their 6-inch guns, were decisively out-ranged. The range, however, was slowly closing owing to the superior speed of the Italian cruisers, who now concentrated their fire on the *Gloucester*. The latter had developed engine trouble the night before but now appeared to have overcome the defect. Though still out-ranged she was able to avoid being hit by "snaking the line".

By 8.29 a.m. the range had fallen to 23,500 yards and *Gloucester* opened fire with her 6-inch guns, firing three salvoes, all of which fell short. *Gloucester*'s salvoes caused the Italian cruisers to alter course away for a few minutes, and when they regained a parallel course at 8.37 they were still out of range of the British cruisers. The Italian salvoes were all falling short. Just before *Gloucester* opened fire, *Vendetta* developed engine trouble. Pridham-Wippell ordered her to return to Alexandria thus reducing his destroyer escort to three.

At 8.55 a.m. the Italian cruisers suddenly ceased fire, and, turning a circle to port, withdrew to the north-westward. In spite of their advantage in speed and range they had scored no hits and had been drawn some fifty miles closer to our battlefleet which was now steaming 310° at 22 knots.

There are few survivors from the senior officers in Pridham-Wippell's force but I have a valuable note written as "hazy recollections" by the Admiral's staff officer operations, Commander R. L. Fisher (now Rear-Admiral R. L. Fisher, C.B.,

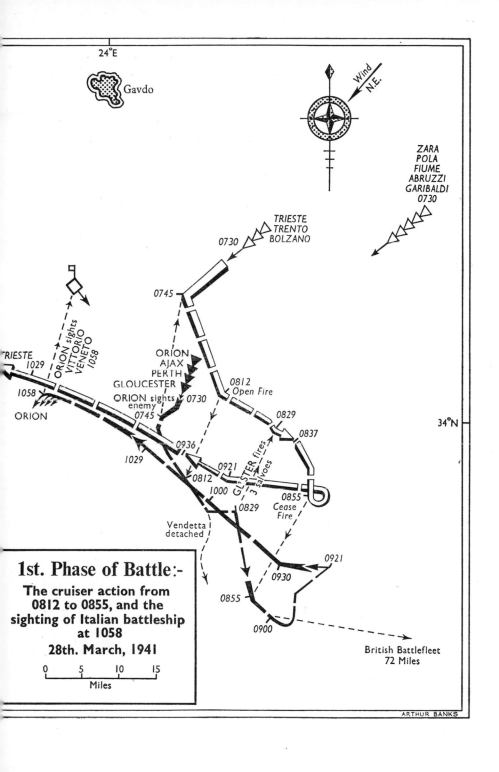

24°E

Gavdo

Wind N.E.

ZARA
POLA
FIUME
ABRUZZI
GARIBALDI
0730

TRIESTE
TRENTO
BOLZANO
0730

0745

ORION sights
VITTORIO
VENETO
1058

TRIESTE
1029

1058

ORION

ORION
AJAX
PERTH
GLOUCESTER
ORION sights
enemy
0745

0730

0812
Open Fire

0829

0837

34°N

0936

1029

0921

0812

GLOSTER fires
3 salvoes

1000

0855
Cease
Fire

0829

Vendetta
detached

0921

0930

0855

0900

British Battlefleet
72 Miles

1st. Phase of Battle:-

**The cruiser action from
0812 to 0855, and the
sighting of Italian battleship
at 1058**

28th. March, 1941

0   5   10   15
Miles

ARTHUR BANKS

D.S.O., O.B.E., D.S.C.) which gives a vivid picture of events as seen from the cruisers. Fisher was an officer who had had considerable seagoing experience, much of it in destroyers.

"My main recollection of the cruisers' part", writes Fisher, "is rather ignominious—we seemed to be always having to run away.

"This is what I remember.

"First thing in the morning I was on the bridge off Gavdo and we saw a small aircraft of a type which somebody said could only have come from an Italian cruiser. Pretty soon after that we saw the *Trento* lot and ran away for all we were worth, our four cruisers in line abreast zig-zagging and making smoke and the four Australian V. & W. destroyers scattered round us. We were shot at for quite a long time and lots of salvoes came close—close enough for us to get some splashes on deck —but nobody hit. It was during this chase that a destroyer on our starboard beam, *Vendetta* I think, was obviously not able to keep up and was steadily dropping bearing. I drew the admiral's attention to this. For her to merely drop astern on our mean line of advance would have meant annihilation for her and on my suggestion we told her to break away and hope she wouldn't be noticed by the enemy.

"During this run away I was mostly in the plot, but whenever I did come out I couldn't see the enemy for smoke. After a time shells stopped splashing around and we went on running away making smoke. After a bit I said to the admiral that I thought it was our duty to keep touch with the enemy at all costs and that we should perhaps stop making smoke, turn back, and see what we could see, but he went on for a bit longer —possibly only a few minutes, it is difficult to remember. At all events when we did turn round the sea was completely empty and I had a slightly guilty feeling."

Gloucester's aircraft had been catapulted at 8.30 a.m. to spot her fall of shot, and at 9.17 a.m. sighted and reported the *Zara* group which, like the *Trieste* group, was now withdrawing to the westward. This report was passed on the wrong frequency, and never got further than the *Gloucester*.

Pridham-Wippell, unaware of this report, received *Formidable*'s aircraft 5F report of three battleships just before the Italian cruisers of the *Trieste* class had ceased fire and withdrawn. As previously stated, however, he considered this report "mani-

8   *Vice-Admiral Sir Henry D. Pridham-Wippell who was in command of the*
British cruisers at Matapan

9　*H.M.A.S. "Perth", H.M.S. "Ajax", and H.M.S. "Orion" at Matapan as seen from H.M.S. "Gloucester"*

10 *A few minutes later. The British cruisers making smoke when under fire: H.M.A.S. "Perth" in foreground, as seen from H.M.S. "Gloucester"*

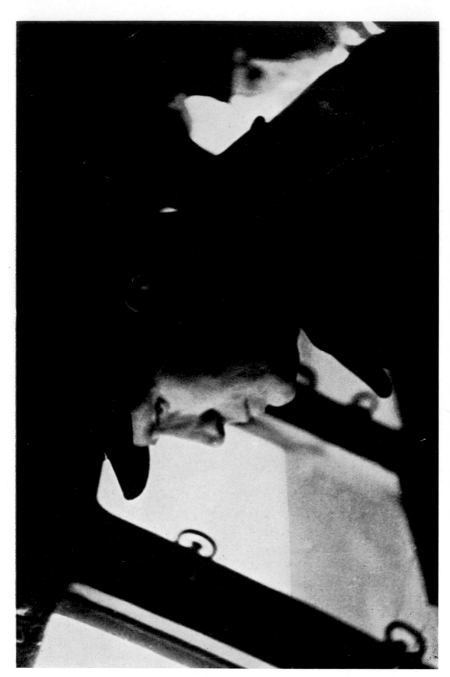

11 *Admiral Angelo Iachino, Commander-in-Chief of the Italian Fleet at Matapan*

festly incorrect" and decided to follow and shadow the ships that had been engaging his force. At 9.36 a.m. he reported the three enemy cruisers and three destroyers still in sight steaming 320° at 28 knots, distant 16 miles from him.

The first round had been fought without either side scoring a hit, and neither side was yet aware of the presence of enemy battleships. Moreover the exact sizes and dispositions of forces generally remained obscure. It was known that the *Garibaldi* class of cruiser bore a similar appearance to the *Cavour* class battleships and it was realised that it would be very difficult to distinguish between the two from the air with certainty. A report of three Italian battleships had been received, yet had been discounted. In fact, as we shall see, the very modern 15-inch battleship *Vittorio Veneto* wearing the flag of Admiral Iachino, Commander-in-Chief of the Italian Fleet, had been only a few miles distant on the port quarter of Pridham-Wippell in *Orion* as he raced to the south-east with the intent of drawing the Italian cruisers within range of the British battlefleet. And now Pridham-Wippell was himself racing to the north-westward, about to fall into the same sort of trap that he had hoped to set the Italians.

It may be interesting to refer to the speed of advance of the British battlefleet. Their position at 7 a.m., 12 hours after leaving harbour, was 240 miles from Alexandria, representing a speed of 20 knots, and this was maintained until 8.27 a.m. when, after receiving *Orion*'s sighting report, the Commander-in-Chief increased to 22 knots. In view of expected sightings and the appointed 6.30 a.m. position for Pridham-Wippell, it might well be asked why the British battlefleet, still 150 miles from the appointed position at 6.30 a.m. on the 28th, had not put on speed during the night. The modernised *Warspite* and *Valiant* were normally capable of a good 24 knots, but the old *Barham* which had not been modernised could scarcely do 23 knots. In the event, however, it was the afore-mentioned condenser trouble in *Warspite* that proved the limiting factor, reducing the maximum speed of the Fleet during the night to 20 knots. Turning into the north-east to fly off *Formidable*'s aircraft at dawn also reduced the speed of advance.

In answer to a question concerning the speed of advance of the battlefleet during the night, Admiral Sir Manley Power, K.C.B., C.B.E., D.S.O., who was staff officer operations to the Commander-in-Chief at the time, explains the position:

> "It must be remembered that we were in no particular hurry as we had not appreciated any threat which was not within the capacity of the cruisers to handle. It was a latish decision that the battlefleet should go to sea at all."

Having ordered an increase to 22 knots at 8.32 a.m., Cunningham, twenty minutes later, ordered *Valiant* to proceed at utmost speed to join Pridham-Wippell whose position under fire from the Italian 8-inch cruisers, though "not unduly alarming", was one which appeared to require instant support. *Nubian* and *Mohawk* were detailed to accompany her for anti-submarine protection. On receiving *Orion*'s sighting report, the Commander-in-Chief had also ordered *Formidable* to range a torpedo striking force but decided to hold it back until he could be certain about the presence, and the exact position, of the Italian battlefleet. He did not want to reveal his strength until he could be certain of catching them.

Cunningham records that the limited speed of *Warspite* was causing him much annoyance, but the matter was now taken in hand by the fleet engineer officer who quickly effected the necessary measures. In a short time *Warspite* was working up to her correct full speed of 24 knots. "I was gratified", Cunningham says, "to see that the *Valiant*, which had been coming up at full speed from astern, was no longer gaining. We pressed on together."

On hearing at 9.18 a.m. that the enemy cruisers had broken off the action with Pridham-Wippell's cruisers, the Commander-in-Chief cancelled the signal ordering *Valiant* ahead at utmost speed, and speed was reduced to 22 knots to allow the *Barham* to keep up. *Nubian* and *Mohawk* were ordered to rejoin the destroyer screen.

All now seemed set for the next move. At some time shortly

to be found appropriate, the Fleet Air Arm would attack and slow up or stop the Italians. This would be followed by the battlefleet arriving for the kill. The stakes seemed enormous. But valuable time had already been lost through *Warspite*'s condenser trouble, and even now the maximum speed was limited to that of the *Barham*. One can imagine that the "caged tiger act" dominated the scene in *Warspite*.

7

Italian Viewpoint

IT IS APPROPRIATE to look for a while at the Italian point of view. The battle has been fully described from the Italian viewpoint in a book called *Gavdo and Matapan*, written in Italian by Admiral A. Iachino, the Commander-in-Chief of the Italian Fleet at the battle of Cape Matapan. The book does not altogether accord with our own views of certain phases or events, but is interesting as a reference, giving as it does the circumstances leading up to the battle, and the thoughts and opinions of the Italian Commander-in-Chief in considerable detail. Throughout, one can sense the bitter regret experienced by Iachino at being so badly served, as he felt, by the air arms of Germany and Italy. It is always difficult to record tracks accurately, owing to discrepancies in assessed positions of ships that are out of visual touch. The finally accepted tracks shown in the diagram (pp. 162–163) can be no more than a compromise of all those rendered with the battle narratives of individual ships, including those given to us by the Italians.

Iachino had been the Italian naval attaché in London from 1931 to 1934, and therefore had a good understanding of British ways. He explains that the concept of a conflict with the British Navy had always been excluded from the practical studies undertaken at the Italian Institute of Warfare, but deplores the fact that Italy failed to establish and maintain her local naval superiority in the early days of the war, beginning with an all-out air and sea attack on Malta. In the absence of definite action, morale gradually waned, and the Italians began to regard themselves as inferior to

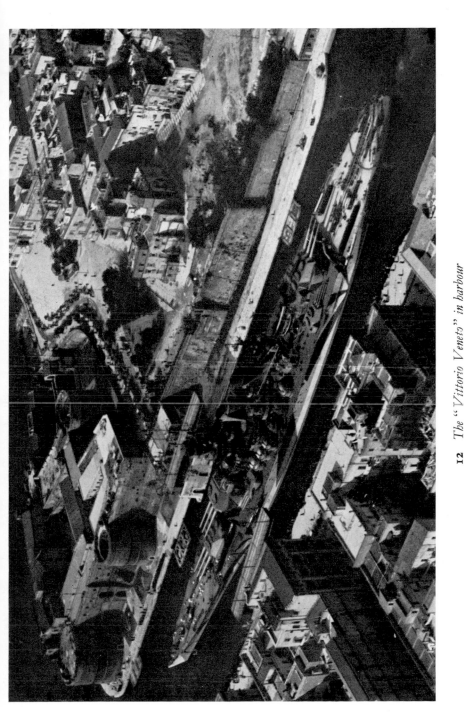

12   The "*Vittorio Veneto*" *in harbour*

13   *The Italian cruiser "Bolzano" of the 3rd Cruiser Division, photographed from
an attacking Swordfish of 815 Squadron*

14   *The Italian cruiser "Zara" of the 1st Cruiser Division*

the British, in spite of their material superiority. By the end of August 1940, Cunningham had strengthened his fleet, and the attack on Taranto in November 1940 had practically put an end to any Italian ideas of aggressive naval measures. This attack, says Iachino, revealed at once the deficiency in Italian long-range reconnaissance aircraft.

On 16th March 1941 Iachino was told that it was absolutely necessary to do something in the Eastern Mediterranean, to intimidate Greece, and to encourage Jugoslavia. This provided for a double offensive sweep, one to the south of Gavdo, the other to the Western Aegean, an area which according to German air reconnaissance was "used daily by important British military convoys".

It was decided that Italy's new battleship the *Vittorio Veneto* should take part. She was very fast for a battleship, and reputed to be capable of $30\frac{1}{2}$ knots. She was also well armed with nine 15-inch guns which were easily superior to the 15-inch guns of the old British battleships. She could therefore overtake and out-range any of our old battleships at her leisure.

Iachino mentions repeatedly his concern about the air co-operation which might be expected from the German bombers and long-range reconnaissance aircraft based in Sicily. Although improvised arrangements were also made for fighter cover to be provided by the Germans, difficulties existed over communications and recognition signals, and apprehension was shown concerning the danger from the air in waters surrounded by British airfields.

It is fairly clear that the objective of the operation was to be no trial of strength, but rather a deterrent to LUSTRE; nevertheless, with the possibility of picking up one or two ripe plums, Iachino's fleet was quite a formidable one. His flagship, the *Vittorio Veneto*, sailed from Naples at 9 p.m. on the 26th March, and was later joined by the *Trieste* class cruisers and *Abruzzi* class cruisers from Brindisi, and the *Zara* class cruisers from Taranto. For convenience his fleet has been grouped as follows:

FORCE Y

One 35,000-ton battleship	*Vittorio Veneto*	Nine 15-inch	Admiral Iachino
Four 1,620-ton destroyers	*Granatiere*	Five 4·7-inch	
	Fuciliere	,,	
	Bersagliere	,,	
	Alpino	,,	

FORCE X

Three 10,000-ton cruisers	*Trieste*	Eight 8-inch	V.-Adm. Sansonetti
	Trento	,,	
	Bolzano	,,	
Three 1,620-ton destroyers	*Corazziere*	Five 4·7-inch	
	Carabiniere	,,	
	Ascari	,,	

FORCE Z

Three 10,000-ton cruisers	*Zara*	Eight 8-inch	V.-Adm. Cattaneo
	Fiume	,,	
	Pola	,,	
Two 7,874-ton cruisers	*Abruzzi*	Ten 6-inch	V.-Adm. Legnani
	Garibaldi	,,	
Four 1,568-ton destroyers	*Gioberti*	Four 4·7-inch	
	Alfieri	,,	
	Oriani	,,	
	Carducci	,,	
Two 1,628-ton destroyers	*Da Recco*	Six 4·7-inch	
	Pessagno	,,	

At 12.25 p.m. on the 27th, *Trieste* signalled Iachino that she had been sighted by a Sunderland aircraft. Iachino shortly afterwards received a deciphered version of the Sunderland's report to Alexandria, and was relieved to find that only three cruisers and a destroyer had been sighted. His course had been reported as 120°, so he altered the course of the fleet to 150° to give the impression that they were bound for Cyrenaica. Mist had prevented the Sunderland from sighting anything more of the fleet, and no further reports were intercepted, but Iachino believed that convoy traffic in the Eastern Mediterranean might be suspended, thus depriving him of his most important objective. Later in the afternoon he received a message from Rhodes which stated that a reconnaissance aircraft had seen in Alexandria harbour three

battleships, two aircraft carriers, and some cruisers at 2 p.m., and, apart from a considerable amount of signal traffic intercepted that evening, considered that all was quiet.

At 4.0 p.m. Iachino ordered all ships back to a course of 130° since there had been no further aircraft sightings of his fleet. By 7.30 p.m. it was already dark, and the weather was fair with a light north-easterly breeze. Iachino increased to 23 knots in accordance with previous orders.

At dawn on the 28th, Iachino's fleet was in three groups on a course 130°, with the *Trieste* class cruisers roughly ten miles on the port bow of *Vittorio Veneto*, and the *Zara* class and *Abruzzi* class cruisers about twenty miles to port of the *Trieste* group. *Vittorio Veneto* catapulted her aircraft at 6 a.m. with orders to sweep an area of 100 miles by 20 miles wide and then land at Leros. *Bolzano*'s aircraft was ordered to look for convoys in the Aegean. If nothing were seen before 7 a.m. Iachino intended calling off the operation as having no purpose and would return to base.

There was great excitement when at 6.43 a.m. *Vittorio Veneto*'s aircraft, an RO43 reconnaissance spotter, reported sighting four cruisers and four destroyers steering to the south-east at 18 knots in a position only fifty miles from the battleship. This would be easy meat for Iachino's enormous fleet. Iachino presumed that there must also be a convoy in the vicinity, and pressed on at 30 knots.

It was at this moment that Pridham-Wippell, shortly after reaching his 6.30 a.m. rendezvous, realised that he had been sighted, and increased speed to 20 knots and steered 200° to turn away from the direction of probable reconnaissance.

Further reports were made by the RO43 which later departed for Rhodes. Iachino complains bitterly at the fact that his aircraft were antiquated and could not be recovered at sea.

Just before eight o'clock, *Trieste* sighted cruisers and reported them as steaming at high speed, evidently bound for Alexandria. At 8.12 a.m. action was joined, as described in the previous chapter, and lasted until 8.55 a.m., when Vice-Admiral Sansonetti in *Trieste* was ordered to break off the engagement and proceed on a course of 300°. At 9 a.m. all Italian ships were steering 300°, and Iachino says that he was still of the opinion that the British battlefleet was in harbour at Alexandria, since he had had no reports to the contrary from his reconnaissance aircraft.

Iachino seems to have been surprised that Pridham-Wippell had withdrawn from Sansonetti and "considering the equality of force had refused to fight". He compares the twenty-four 8-inch guns of the three Italian cruisers with the thirty-six 6-inch guns of the four British cruisers, but seems to discount the fact that the Italian cruisers with their higher speed could, in theory at any rate, choose a range which would always be to their advantage. If, then, he was expecting the British cruisers to fight, it seems odd that he should not have looked for some other reason for their retirement at speed to the south-east. He continued to refuse to believe in the possibility of the British battlefleet being at sea in support of the cruisers, though he was aware that Pridham-Wippell was now following Sansonetti at a discreet distance as they withdrew to the north-west.

Soon after 9.0 a.m. he received the following message from Rhodes:

> "At 0745 No. 1 aircraft of the Aegean strategic reconnaissance sighted 1 carrier 2 battleships 9 cruisers 14 destroyers in sector 3836/0 course 165° 20 knots"

Iachino had himself been in this position at 7.45 a.m. and assumed at once that it was his own force that had been reported. He immediately informed Rhodes that a gross blunder had been perpetrated. He now thought up a scheme for the annihilation of Pridham-Wippell's force.

Iachino had not himself sighted the British cruisers but knew from reports from Sansonetti that the latter was being shadowed by Pridham-Wippell. He estimated that the British cruisers were some distance to the south of *Vittorio Veneto*, and therefore at 10.30 a.m. ordered his battleship to alter course to the eastward with the intention of working round to the northward of the British cruisers and taking up station just out of sight on their starboard quarter. As soon as he was in this advantageous

15   *No. 815 Squadron Swordfish attack on "Bolzano" at noon, 28th March 1941*

16   *H.M.S. " Hasty " straddled by enemy gunfire at Matapan*

position he intended ordering Sansonetti to reverse course and double back on his shadowers, thus driving them into the full fury of the 15-inch guns of *Vittorio Veneto*.

Pridham-Wippell's four 6-inch cruisers were to be sandwiched between Sansonetti's three 8-inch cruisers and a 15-inch battleship: an unhappy fate.

8

Sandwich Operation

MEANWHILE in the British Fleet the exact constitution and disposition of the Italian Fleet was still obscure. Messages continued to come in, but no report of battleships was received other than that which had been sent by *Formidable*'s aircraft 5F at 8.05 a.m. reporting three enemy battleships.

In *Formidable* we were still proceeding at 22 knots to the north-westward and at 8.33 a.m. had been ordered to range a torpedo striking force. The north-easterly wind had moderated, but *Formidable* would still be required to turn into wind for flying off: which would thus delay our speed of advance. Visibility was now very good and the sea calm; the latest weather map indicated continuing fine or fair weather and the probability of a wind from the north-west by afternoon. If the latter materialised much valuable time would be saved. There seemed to be little immediate hope of a surface action unless enemy ships could be slowed down. We remained in a state of first readiness for action, all our 4.5-inch guns and pom-poms manned to repel any air attack.

Lieutenant-Commander Gerald Saunt, the commanding officer of 826 Squadron, was to lead the torpedo striking force consisting of six Albacores each armed with a 40-knot Mark 12 torpedo, with a depth setting of 34 feet. A last-minute change to 28 feet was made in three of these when it became doubtful that an enemy battleship was present, and it was thought that the targets would almost certainly be cruisers. Names of aircraft crews in the *Formidable*'s strikes are given in Appendix V. An escort of two Fulmar fighters belonging to 803 Squadron was to accompany the striking force. The Albacores were single-engined biplanes with a top speed of 143 knots and an economical speed of 92 knots. In practice, however, when armed with a torpedo or a 1,500-lb bomb, and carrying the full crew of pilot, observer, and gunner, and faced with a long endurance run of four or five hours, their effective speed was probably less than 90 knots. The Fulmars were single-engined monoplanes with a top speed of 222 knots at 10,000 feet and an economical speed of 150 knots at the same height. They carried a pilot and observer and were armed with eight 0·303-inch cannon. Their endurance was also of the order of four or five hours but could be much less when engaged in high-speed combat. Once airborne there was always much uncertainty about return. With a deterioration of visibility or an increase of swell, landing conditions could be precarious. Even when the carrier had been found, on return from a strike or search, it might not be possible to land on for some time either because another force was already ranged on deck, or because turning into wind was impracticable at the moment in view of manœuvring restrictions or imminence of aircraft attack. In this connection one of the most difficult decisions in carrier handling at that time was to decide on the crucial moment for the fighters to take off. There was no point in keeping them back until the last minute as they could not gain sufficient height in time. On the other hand it was imprudent to commit too many to the air at an early stage if a large-scale attack could be expected later. Under certain circumstances the catapult or assisted take off could be used for a fighter, but normally the delay of turning the carrier into wind had to be accepted.

The striking force had been ordered to range aircraft at 8.33 a.m. at the moment that our cruisers were being engaged by the Italians, and these aircraft were shortly afterwards being fuelled, armed with torpedoes, and having engines run up on the after part of the flight deck. The crews came up to the briefing room in the island, where they were given the latest information, such as we had, on enemy dispositions, and wind and weather. At 9.22 a.m., however, after news had been received that the enemy

71

cruisers had broken off action with Pridham-Wippell, the Commander-in-Chief decided to hold them back for a while. His main concern was the slowness of his own battleships. Before revealing the presence of a British carrier, and possibly battle-ships, by a Fleet Air Arm attack, he wished to be sure of being near enough to be able to overtake and destroy any enemy ship that might be slowed down by such an attack.

As a diversion which would not affect the readiness of *Formidable*'s strike the Commander-in-Chief made a signal at 8.49 a.m. to the naval air station at Maleme at the western end of Crete, ordering a torpedo striking force to attack enemy cruisers which had been in position 33° 50′ North 24° 14′ East at 8.12 a.m. steering 100°. These were the *Trieste* cruisers which were at that time chasing our own cruisers. The signal had to be made to H.M.S. *York* for onward transmission to Maleme and was not received until 10.05 a.m. *York* was lying beached in Suda Bay at Crete, having been damaged by an explosive motor boat two days earlier.

A signal was also made to Royal Air Force 201 Group at 9.25 a.m. to send flying boats to locate and shadow the enemy fleet.

Maleme had already that morning flown off four Swordfish armed with torpedoes, and had searched the area west of Crete without sighting anything. One of these had suffered engine trouble, but all returned to Maleme by 8.45 a.m. On receipt of the Commander-in-Chief's message at 10.05 a.m., three of these Swordfish again flew off at 10.50 a.m., having been refuelled and armed with Mark 12 torpedoes. Flying at 9,000 feet they reached the vicinity of the *Trieste* group at noon and sighted them steering 300° at 28 to 30 knots. Five minutes later they made a torpedo attack on the rear cruiser, the *Bolzano*, approaching from out of the sun towards the cruiser's port quarter. The ships all took avoiding action and each torpedo missed. In spite of anti-aircraft fire from the cruisers the aircraft escaped damage and returned safely to Maleme.

Let us now follow the movements of *Formidable*'s aircraft. A decision had been made in the flagship not to delay the

17   *Salvo falling ahead of H.M.S. "Gloucester"*

18   *Salvo partially obscuring H.M.S. "Gloucester"*

19   *H.M.S. "Gloucester" laying a smoke screen*

20 *An Albacore, having just dropped its torpedo*

21 *The Albacore turning violently away*

carrier's strike any longer. As will be seen this was a providential decision. After receipt of a signal from the Commander-in-Chief, *Formidable* at 9.56 a.m. turned into wind and flew off her first striking force of six Albacores and two Fulmars. A Swordfish of 826 Squadron took off at the same time for action observation, duty J.

At 9.59 a.m. the Commander-in-Chief made the following signal to Vice-Admiral Light Forces:

"Torpedo striking force on its way."

This must have been read by Pridham-Wippell to mean that an enemy force was about to attack him, for between 10.45 a.m. and 11.00 a.m. when Saunt's Albacores reached the target area, the British cruisers fired on them.

Saunt's observer, Lieutenant Hopkins (now Rear-Admiral F. H. E. Hopkins, D.S.O., D.S.C.) writes of the attack:

> "I remember that we were briefed to go out and attack Italian cruisers some eighty miles ahead of the Fleet. We set off with six Albacores, armed with torpedoes, and were escorted by two Fulmar fighters. On reaching the target area we passed four British cruisers steaming in line ahead. In spite of our repeated attempts to identify ourselves to them they kept up a steady barrage of A.A. fire at us until we eventually passed out of range ahead of them."

At this moment Pridham-Wippell was following hard on the heels of Sansonetti unaware of the grim fate which Iachino had planned for him, and in fact unaware of Iachino's presence at all.

> "We now steamed westward again", continues Fisher, "feeling braver and braver as we recovered from our first plastering. It was sunny and the sea was void of enemy; the turret crews were sitting on the roofs of their turrets, and action bully beef sandwiches arrived on the bridge. The commander (T. C. Wynne) came on the bridge and, with his mouth full of sandwich, nudged me and said, 'What battleship is that over on the starboard beam? I thought ours were miles to the east of us.' As I took my binoculars to examine a vessel hull down to the northward there was a whistling noise and the first salvo of 15-inch from the *Vittorio Veneto* landed somewhere around. We made a very hurried turn to the south (I think without waiting for our turn signal to be answered), and did another hurried retreat making smoke."

The official report describes the event with more gravity, and says that the position took a critically dramatic turn at 10.58 a.m. when a look-out in *Orion* suddenly sighted an unknown vessel to the northward bearing 002° at a distance of 16 miles. (See diagram opposite.) A minute later the ship had been identified as one of the *Vittorio Veneto* class of battleship. At the same moment she opened fire with her 15-inch guns on *Orion*. Pridham-Wippell immediately altered course to the southward and increased to full speed, 30 knots. Cunningham in *Warspite* was electrified at this moment to receive three intercepted emergency signals made by Pridham-Wippell to his cruisers:

> "Make smoke by all available means."
> "Turn together to 180 degrees."
> "Proceed at your utmost speed."

It was now obvious to Cunningham that the enemy battlefleet had been sighted, and excitement was intense.

> "As the signals came in," writes Barnard, "there was the usual chat among the lower orders of the staff—'Hallo, what's up?' —'What on earth is V.A.L.F. up to?'. ABC took one look at the signals and said 'Don't be so damn silly. He's sighted the enemy battlefleet, and if you'd ever done any reasonable time in destroyers, you'd know it without waiting for the amplifying report. Put the enemy battlefleet in at visibility distance to the northward of him.' A few minutes later the confirming report arrived."

There was some anxiety for the *Gloucester*, whose engine trouble had considerably reduced her maximum safe speed. The fire from the battleship, however, acted as drastic tonic and *Gloucester* seemed to have no difficulty in keeping up with the remainder of Pridham-Wippell's force as they raced at full speed towards the south in an attempt to escape annihilation.

At 11 a.m. Sansonetti altered course to port with his *Trieste* division, in accordance with Iachino's plan for him to engage Pridham-Wippell from the starboard quarter.

Pridham-Wippell was now in a perilous position, pursued by Sansonetti, who with his superior speed would shortly be within

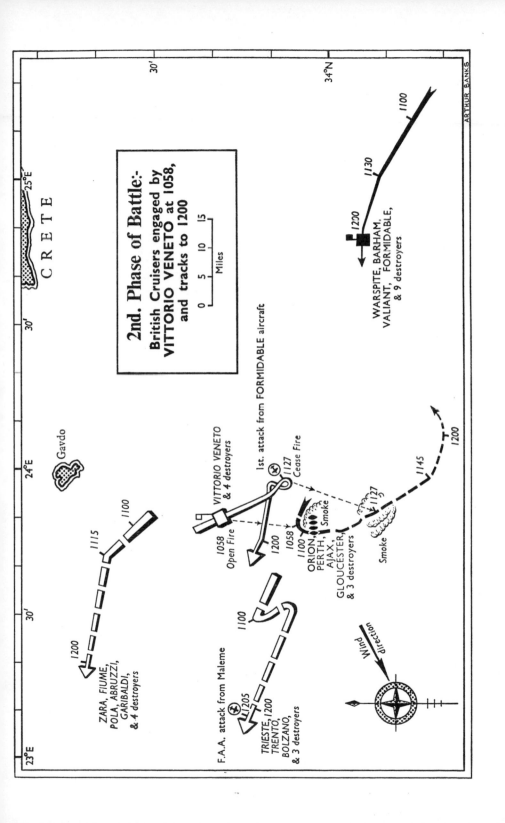

2nd. Phase of Battle:-
British Cruisers engaged by
VITTORIO VENETO at 1058,
and tracks to 1200

Miles
0 5 10 15

C R E T E

25°E
30'
24°E
30'
23°E

30'
34°N

Gavdo

ZARA, FIUME,
POLA, ABRUZZI,
GARIBALDI,
& 4 destroyers

1200
1115
1100

VITTORIO VENETO
& 4 destroyers

1st. attack from FORMIDABLE aircraft

1058
Open Fire
1200
1058
1100
1127
Cease Fire

ORION,
PERTH,
AJAX,
GLOUCESTER,
& 3 destroyers
Smoke
1127
Smoke

1145
1200

F.A.A. attack from Maleme
1100
1205

TRIESTE, 1200
TRENTO,
BOLZANO,
& 3 destroyers

Wind
direction

WARSPITE, BARHAM,
VALIANT, FORMIDABLE,
& 9 destroyers

1200
1130
1100

ARTHUR BANKS

range of him, and being fired on by *Vittorio Veneto* who found no difficulty in keeping up with him. The range was about 12 miles, and the battleship's fire was accurate. She now concentrated on *Orion* and soon scored a near miss which caused *Orion* some minor damage. Pridham-Wippell had ordered his force to make smoke, and with the wind light from the north-east, this began to be effective as a screen. Only one ship, the *Gloucester*, remained visible to the enemy who quickly shifted fire to her and repeatedly straddled her with 15-inch shell. The destroyer *Hasty* moved into position to close the gap and make smoke which soon effectively hid the *Gloucester* from the *Vittorio Veneto*. With the approach of Sansonetti on Pridham-Wippell's starboard quarter, however, the position remained desperate. At this critical moment, 11.27 a.m., when all might have seemed lost, *Formidable*'s striking force arrived.

Hopkins writes:

> "We sighted one large warship, escorted by four destroyers, steaming towards our cruisers, and shortly after this the large warship, which turned out to be a battleship of the *Littorio* class, opened fire on our cruisers. Since the battleship was steaming at 30 knots, it was clear that our cruisers were in for trouble, and they could expect no help from the main fleet which was more than eighty miles away.
>
> "At about this time two German JU88 fighter bombers dived out of the sun into our formation. They were at once spotted by our two Fulmars (piloted by Lieutenant Donald Gibson and Petty Officer Theobold). One was shot down in flames, and the other fled."

Gibson, now a captain, writes:

> "Petty Officer Theobold and I shot down a Junkers 88 on the way in, escorting Saunt's squadron. It was a head on attack we made and we did not see him hit the sea, but Pinky Haworth did. Later we straffed the *Vittorio Veneto*, but quite out of phase with the torpedo attack; early I think."

Gibson ends:

> "P.O. Theobold died in his bed in 1956. A record for 803 Squadron."

78

22 *Salvo from the " Vittorio Veneto "*

23   The poop of the " *Vittorio Veneto* " after her reconnaissance plane had been damaged by own gunfire

Hopkins continues:

> "It now became obvious that unless we could do something quickly our cruisers would be picked off one by one at long range by the *Vittorio*. The trouble was that we were all abaft the beam of *Vittorio*, she was steaming at 30 knots, the wind at our height was 30 knots against us, so that since our air speed was only 90 knots we were catching up at a relative speed of only 30 knots. I think it took the best part of twenty minutes to creep up to a suitable attacking position ahead of *Vittorio*. Throughout most of this time she and her four destroyers kept up a spirited but fortunately inaccurate bombardment with their A.A. guns. The battleship was also doing some good shooting at our cruisers and appeared to be straddling them frequently. I suspect that the only reason that they did not score any direct hits was that the spread of their individual salvoes was too large.
>
> "Eventually we got into an attacking position and the first flight of three aircraft dived to the starboard bow of the target and dropped torpedoes. As the *Vittorio* turned to comb the tracks she was caught beam on by the second flight of three aircraft. At least one torpedo hit and *Vittorio* circled through 360° and apparently stopped. She also ceased fire on the cruisers. After a while she got under way and steamed off to the north-west breaking off the action with our cruisers."

Saunt was also convinced that *Vittorio Veneto* had received at least one hit, probably more, and reported this on return to *Formidable*.

It is interesting to read Iachino's account of the action. We last left him proceeding eastward to get round to the northward of Pridham-Wippell, to carry out his plan for an annihilating sandwich operation. To his surprise, he found that the British cruisers were considerably to the northward of the estimated position, and the sighting took place much sooner than expected, the cruisers appearing broad on his starboard bow steaming a course opposite to Iachino's. The four British cruisers were closing rapidly when sighted and the leading ship was seen to flash a challenge. Iachino's reply was to open fire. The range from *Vittorio Veneto* was 23,000 metres at that time, 10.58 a.m. Orders were immediately sent to Sansonetti's 3rd Cruiser Division to reverse course and engage the British cruisers. Iachino described how the

British ships altered hurriedly to the southward and began to make thick black smoke, each ship snaking the line of fire by alterations of 30° of course. They opened fire on him but soon found they were outranged and ceased fire. *Vittorio Veneto* continued to engage, finding the ships well within range but obscured most of the time by smoke.

Iachino goes on to say how cheered he was when, at 11 a.m., a look-out from the mast-head reported sighting six aircraft which looked like Italian CR43 escorts. These must be the planes from Rhodes for which he had waited so long. His joy was short lived for the air liaison officer amended his first appreciation and said that the planes were British. The battleship and all the destroyers in company opened up with anti-aircraft guns and machine-guns. Iachino saw the aircraft drop six torpedoes but considered the dropping zone in each case to be more than 2,000 metres from *Veneto*. In spite of Saunt's conviction that there had been at least one hit, all torpedoes missed *Veneto*, and, according to Iachino passed astern. The attack, however, had saved the British cruisers from annihilation for *Veneto* broke off the action and steamed towards the north-west. The sandwich operation had been foiled.

From the official record it is evident that the *Vittorio Veneto* received no hits in this particular attack, but had a narrow escape. Our aircraft, flying at 9,000 feet, manœuvred to reach a position out of the sun on the starboard bow of the battleship, and away from her destroyer escort, and then at 11.27 a.m. attacked in two waves. When the first sub-flight was at 1,000 feet, *Vittorio Veneto* altered course through more than 120° to starboard. Two of the aircraft of the first sub-flight, already committed to the attack, dropped their torpedoes when on the starboard side, and the third from fine on the starboard bow. Taking advantage of the *Vittorio Veneto*'s turn the second sub-flight dropped torpedoes from good positions on her port bow as she was turning. All six tracks passed clear, two ahead, four astern.

Pridham-Wippell, racing southwards at full speed under a smoke screen, failed to see the air attack that had arrived at such an opportune moment. Nor did he see *Vittorio Veneto* turn away, eventually resuming course to the north-westward, or Sansonetti doing likewise at high speed. As the smoke cleared he could only see a clear horizon to the northward where the *Vittorio Veneto* had been and to the north-westward where the *Trieste* division had a few minutes earlier been bearing down upon him.

Pridham-Wippell altered course to gain touch with Cunningham. At 12.24 p.m. *Gloucester* sighted the screen of the British battlefleet bearing 046°.

Iachino reports that during the action with Pridham-Wippell's force, which lasted half an hour, the range varied between 23,000 and 26,000 metres. *Vittorio Veneto* fired ninety-four 15-inch shells in twenty-nine salvoes. Of these, eleven shells were faulty, and though they straddled the target repeatedly and there were many near misses, and "the usual claims of observers that they had seen definite hits and orange flames from the resulting fires", there was not a single hit.

The Italian Fleet now proceeded on its course 300° towards home at 28 knots.

In the meantime Cunningham, now only 45 miles to the east-south-east, was chasing hopefully at top speed: a top speed, however, that would be quite insufficient, as it came to be realised, unless the Italian ships could be slowed down by further aircraft attacks.

9

The Chase

Formidable had a total of only twenty-seven aircraft available on board: thirteen Fulmars, ten Albacores (of which only five were fitted with long range tanks), and four Swordfish. These had to cover all routine requirements, such as fighter protection and anti-submarine patrol in addition to the shadowing, mass reconnaissance, and offensive strikes needed in battle. A reference to *Formidable's* log for this day* will show that flying operations were conducted on twenty-one separate occasions. Of these, five were the big occasions when the larger parties such as the dawn search and the striking forces were handled. The remainder were the relatively smaller occasions when it was necessary to despatch or accept aircraft allocated for fighter patrol, anti-submarine patrol, or observation duties. Each operation might occupy only a few minutes but required an alteration of course into the wind which was upsetting when the whole fleet had to conform to these movements to ensure that the destroyer screen would remain effective. The essential routine operations severely limited the number of aircraft that could be made ready and available for the big parties. A dawn search and torpedo strike had already been carried out, nevertheless a second torpedo striking force was fuelled, armed, and ranged, and was ready for take off shortly before noon. This consisted of three Albacores and two Swordfish from 829 Squadron and was to be led by the commanding officer of the squadron, Lieutenant-Commander Dalyell-Stead, posthumously awarded the D.S.O. for his gallantry on this day.

* See Appendix IV.

84

Two Fulmars from 803 Squadron were to accompany them. This was a pitiably small force for such an important attack, especially when compared with the large forces of attacking aircraft which were available in our carriers in the Pacific Campaign of 1945. One of the Albacores of this group had landed on as recently as 11.32 a.m. Another Albacore, the 5B aircraft that had made the first enemy sighting report at 7.20 a.m., had found difficulty in locating *Formidable*, and being short of petrol made for Egypt and finally landed at Bardia.

The first striking force returned to *Formidable* between noon and 12.15 p.m. after attacking *Vittorio Veneto* and claiming, as they then thought, a probable hit. *Formidable* was now detached with two destroyers, to conduct her flying operations independently from the fleet and so allow the battleships to continue the chase at the maximum speed of the fleet. This maximum was limited by the *Barham* to about 22 knots, but it was thought that the Italian battleship had been slowed down by the hits claimed by Saunt's squadron. As we turned into wind we quickly dropped astern of the battlefleet.

The sun was now shining and accentuated the black, white, and grey camouflage of the great forms of *Warspite*, *Barham*, and *Valiant*, steaming at speed in line ahead away from us, each with a magnificent white bow wave and a glistening wake, each with eight powerful 15-inch guns trained fore and aft. The question in all our minds was whether these guns would be in action before the end of the day, firing shells which weighed approximately a ton each. Their white ensigns contrasted with the cobalt of the sky and the ultramarine of the sea. The leading ship, the *Warspite*, flew the flag of the Commander-in-Chief at the mainmast: a red cross on a white background. The third ship, the *Barham*, flew the flag of the rear-admiral of the first battle squadron: the red cross of St. George defaced by a red ball in each of the inner quadrants. The three battleships were but a remnant of the Grand Fleet that had sailed the seas with great majesty at Jutland in 1916, nevertheless they presented a striking scene of power and grandeur. As they rapidly withdrew towards the horizon we in *Formidable* began to feel somewhat defenceless in the absence of their heavy guns. We were reassured at the thought of the Italian Fleet legging it for home fifty or sixty miles to the northwest of our battlefleet. The first striking force "stacked up" in the air meanwhile and awaited instructions to land on. Dalyell-Stead's squadron and escorting fighters, having been effectively briefed, now flew off. We watched them race along the flight deck, and wished them luck as they took off. As soon as those of 829 Squadron were clear, 826 Squadron were directed to fly on. Guided by Simon Borrett waving his bats, they landed on one by one and came to a halt under the sudden restraining influence of the arrester wires. We were relieved to see them all return. The observers came up to the briefing room in the island, and told their story. They told of the *Vittorio Veneto*'s sudden alteration of course 120° to starboard as the first sub-flight reached 1,000 feet. They spoke of intense opposition in the shape of light and heavy anti-aircraft fire and a fierce splash barrage. The first sub-flight were already committed to their attack when *Vittorio Veneto* turned, so they had released torpedoes on her starboard side as already described. The second sub-flight then took advantage of the battleship's turn and attacked from ahead broad on the port bow. Saunt, as has been said, claimed at least one probable hit by his force, and, although we know now that this was incorrect, we were greatly encouraged at the time. *Vittorio Veneto* had been slowed down, we thought, and our battlefleet would catch up with them before nightfall. It all looked promising.

At 12.44 p.m. flying on had been completed, and *Formidable* shaped course at full speed to rejoin the battlefleet now out of sight over the horizon. This seemed to be a good time for a meal. Mess teams brought round hot tea and sandwiches to those who could not leave their action stations. There were large blue patches of sky and a strong sun brightened the scene. The sea was calm, and the setting so peaceful that it seemed hard to realise that two powerful opposing fleets were within a few miles of each other, the one racing for the security of its own harbours, unaware that it was being chased by three British battleships, the other straining every nerve to catch up with it. A report from a Royal Air Force bomber came in, reporting two Italian battleships and three cruisers several miles to the north-west of the position in which we imagined the *Vittorio Veneto* to be. This in fact was the group of three of the *Zara* division with the two *Abruzzi* cruisers that looked so much like battleships of the *Cavour* class.

All seemed tranquil as we steamed at high speed to rejoin the Commander-in-Chief. Suddenly the peace was shattered by a loud voice. "Alarm starboard! Enemy aircraft! Green two-five!"

The voice came from the Captain who was the first to spot this aircraft. He pointed briskly at it, and all of us on the compass platform could now see it, low down on the horizon, fine on the starboard bow, coming in fast. The bomber was an Italian S79 and had come in very low. Now it was not much more than 2,000 yards from the ship, and still heading towards us. There was pandemonium on the compass platform as the alarm was repeated into various voicepipes, but outside all was surprisingly quiet, apart from the soft shudder and vibration and the thrash of the bow wave as *Formidable* hurtled along at 30 knots. None of the gun crews seemed to see the rapidly approaching aircraft. Forward of the bridge were two multiple pom-poms ("Chicago pianos"), both fully manned and ready, but uncannily silent. The Captain swore, leaned forward over the dodger, and pointed towards the aircraft which was now little more than 1,000 yards away. The gun crews returned hurt looks. They appeared to be somewhat abashed.

"Wake up!" shouted the Captain. "Look! Over there! Fire at the b-gg-rs!"

For a second, or perhaps two, the crews still seemed nonplussed. Then they cottoned on. With an ear-shattering staccato blast they both opened fire. Every gun in the ship joined in. The aircraft, now broad on the starboard bow, dropped a torpedo, and, wheeling sharply, rapidly opened distance from the ship.

"Hard a starboard" shouted Bisset.

We listed heavily as *Formidable* answered the helm. Quickly she swung to starboard. The Captain then steadied on a course parallel to the direction from which the torpedo had been dropped. The aircraft was now practically out of sight on the horizon. As *Formidable* combed the track we counted the seconds from the dropping time. At a relative speed of approach of about 70 knots, and a range of 1,000 yards, the torpedo would hit or miss 25 seconds after being dropped. Before this time had elapsed there was a further alarm.

"Alarm starboard! Enemy aircraft! Green two-o!"

It was the Captain again. A second S79 was coming in fine on the starboard bow. The aircraft was instantly met by a hostile fire from every gun forward. It dropped a torpedo, and turned fiercely away.

"Hard a starboard!" yelled the Captain. *Formidable* again listed heavily. This time the dropping range had been about 1,500 yards. Anxiously we counted the seconds waiting for the hit that could put us right out of the action. The seconds crawled by. Within the minute we realised we were out of danger. Course was once again resumed to join the battleships.

At 11 a.m., when he first intercepted Pridham-Wippell's emergency signals, Cunningham had had great hopes of bringing the aggressor to action, for the latter, while chasing the British cruisers, was also closing the British battlefleet at high speed. In anticipation of imminent action *Warspite*'s two Swordfish float-planes were catapulted at about 12.15 p.m. for action observation and gunnery spotting duties respectively. Barnard, the fleet gunnery officer, writes:

"During the period 12.00–12.30 daylight contact with the enemy battlefleet appeared imminent; our battlefleet had assumed the first degree of readiness in all respects, with turrets trained to the northward, and it appeared from the plot that the enemy were chasing V.A.L.F. towards us, so that the opposing fleets were closing at some 50 knots and due to make visual contact about 12.40. The destroyer screen was sent ahead to form on their Captains (D), and a high degree of expectancy prevailed. Only once before in the Mediterranean had we sighted the enemy battlefleet in daylight—on the notable occasion off Calabria, in July 1940, when the *Warspite* alone with

25 (*Pages 90–1 following*) H.M.S. "*Formidable*" *seen from the quarter deck of H.M.S.*"*Warspite*"

24 *Italian look-out on the morning of 28th March 1941*

26　H.M.S. *"Orion"*, *Vice-Admiral Pridham-Wippell's flagship*

27　H.M.S. *"Warspite"*, *Admiral Cunningham's flagship*

28　H.M.S. *"Jervis"*, *Captain Mack's flotilla leader*

four 6-inch cruisers had seen the entire Italian Fleet come up over the horizon and deploy as for a peace-time tactical exercise. Off Calabria we had waited until too late before catapulting spotting aircraft, as a result of which the *Warspite*'s first aircraft was caught on the catapult when the first salvo fired. With that bitter memory in his mind, the fleet gunnery officer on this occasion begged to get spotting aircraft off in plenty of time, and off they went, just as an ominous silence was beginning to fall on the plot.

"By 12.25 there was still no news either of V.A.L.F. or the enemy battlefleet, and the doubt was not resolved until 12.30 when V.A.L.F's 'lost-touch' signal, timed 12.10, was received, simultaneously with sighting of V.A.L.F's force on a somewhat unexpected bearing on the port bow. There appears to have been a discrepancy of some ten miles in the reference positions of our two forces.

"It was not until about 12.50 that it became clear that the enemy battleship had turned back to the westward as a result of the naval aircraft attack which had been launched to assist V.A.L.F. out of an awkward situation. So we were back again in the normally-to-be-expected Mediterranean situation of attempting to catch a much faster enemy with a good start on his way home. It was a bitter anti-climax, and no prudent staff officer approached the 'caged tiger' without good cause, while signals were being made for the *Warspite* to reduce speed to enable *Barham* to catch up. There was, however, plenty of daylight left, and a fair hope that the air striking forces might slow down the enemy before dark."

But let us follow the movements of the fleet observer, Lieutenant-Commander Bolt, now Rear-Admiral A. S. Bolt, C.B., D.S.O., D.S.C., who writes:

"I see from my flying log that I was first catapulted from *Warspite* at 12.15, and that the flight actually lasted 4 hours 40 minutes. The main forces were meeting at high speed. The battlefleet steaming to support the cruiser squadron at 23 knots was expected to make contact with the advanced units of the Italian Fleet within at most two hours when *Warspite* launched my aircraft for action observation. My duties were to obtain a visual link between the fleets as soon as possible and then to report generally on the tactical situation as seen from the air.

"During my briefing before take off no instructions had been given to me about recovery at sea at the end of the patrol or returning to Suda Bay. I knew that the second aircraft had been instructed to return to Suda Bay and I assumed that I would be given orders in the air according to the wishes of the Commander-in-Chief in the light of the tactical situation. In H.M.S. *Warspite*, the flag captain assumed that the necessary orders for the aircraft's return to base would be given by the chief of staff.

"The fleets did not make contact as expected, the Italian main force showing no inclination to press on to the south-east after the Fleet Air Arm torpedo attack. The safe endurance of my aircraft was about 4¾ hours, though we had on occasion achieved 5 hours under favourable conditions. My routine reports of fuel state evoked no response from H.M.S. *Warspite* until I reported only 15 minutes of fuel remaining. Suda Bay was over one hour's flying away, so a decision had to be made to recover or destroy the aircraft. In the event the Commander-in-Chief decided to recover the aircraft although the fleet was in hot pursuit of the *Vittorio Veneto*, having been slowed as we thought by a torpedo hit from an aircraft from *Formidable*. My aircraft was ordered to alight ahead of the *Warspite* in the grain of the fleet. With the crane swung out on the starboard side the plan was to hook on as the ship steamed up to overtake the aircraft taxying on a parallel course. The sea was calm and my pilot, P.O. Rice, made a good landing about two cables ahead of the ship, turned on to a parallel course and taxied at about 10 knots with the ship coming up fast astern. We had never practised this method of recovery and were a good deal disturbed by the bow wave. However, I was able to con P.O. Rice to a position under the grab hook and Lieutenant Commander Copeman (now 4th Sea Lord) with whom I had a good understanding in the recovery operation, hoisted us quickly clear of the water as soon as I gave the hooked-on signal. The aircraft was put on the catapult and refuelled while I went to make my peace on the Admiral's bridge. The ship lost only one mile through the water during the recovery and I do not believe she was doing less than 18 knots through the water at any moment during the operation."

Cunningham had altered the course of the battlefleet from 300° to 290° at 11.35 a.m., and from 290° to 270° at noon, hoping soon to overtake *Vittorio Veneto*, who by all accounts had been slowed down. The British battlefleet was still only making good 22 knots. Although the Italian Fleet was being shadowed, and reported by our aircraft, the apparently contradictory nature of some of the reports, due to the fact that there were three separate groups of Italian ships widely separated, made it difficult to obtain a convincing plot. Little by little, however, it became clear that, far from our overtaking the Italians, we were beginning to lag behind. From Iachino's account we know now that he was steaming 300° at 28 knots until 2.0 p.m., at which time he reduced to 25 knots to conserve fuel in his destroyers.

At 12.30 p.m. Cunningham altered back to 290°. Two minutes before this *Jervis* sighted *Orion* on a bearing of 210° and almost instantaneously *Orion* sighted Cunningham's destroyer screen. Pridham-Wippell, having now made visual touch with the British Fleet, amended his reference position, which was found to be 10 miles different from that of the Commander-in-Chief. At 1.05 p.m. he was ordered to proceed ahead with his four cruisers, and to keep station ahead of the battlefleet on a bearing of 290° at maximum visual signalling distance.

Fisher describes the junction with the battlefleet and indicates that their reception was not quite the cordial welcome which they had hoped for from the Commander-in-Chief.

> "It must have been at the end of this retreat", continues Fisher, "that we sighted our Commander-in-Chief, rather unexpectedly, and a discrepancy between Craske's reckoning and Tom Brownrigg's came to light. I can't remember how much it was—10 or 15 miles perhaps—but it was very troublesome when we came to marry up our track charts with that of the Commander-in-Chief afterwards. Much midnight oil was spent on this and you can take it that in the official track some distortion had been resorted to to make them fit. I recollect that Craske and I were quite certain ours was right and Tom Brownrigg's wrong, but we had to distort ours in deference to the Commander-in-Chief's seniority.
>
> "As far as I remember there was an exchange with the Commander-in-Chief on the following lines when we met:
>
> "'Where is the enemy?'
>
> "'Sorry don't know; haven't seen them for some time.'"

The remainder of the exchange implies that Fisher believed they were out of favour, for they were soon sent off ahead again to continue the search. Cunningham makes it quite clear that this was not so. "I was quite satisfied with V.A.L.F.'s operations and actions", he writes.

"All the afternoon we padded away to the westward," continues Fisher, "opening distance from the Commander-in-Chief, and once again feeling braver and braver as we recovered."

Formidable rejoined the battlefleet at 2 p.m. The fleet now presented a powerful spectacle with four 6-inch cruisers in the van at about sixteen miles ahead of the fleet, three 15-inch battleships and an armoured fleet carrier, with thirteen destroyers in attendance. The weather was still fine, with a clear sky, the sea calm, and the wind had moderated and backed to the north-west. This meant that *Formidable* could now fly on and fly off her aircraft without much alteration of course, and the chase could continue without interruption at a steady speed of over 22 knots.

Owing to *Formidable*'s shortage of aircraft, shadowing touch with the enemy had temporarily been lost. By 2 p.m., however, three of the Albacores that had flown on with the return of the first striking force had been refuelled and ranged, and took off to locate and shadow the enemy again. An hour later, Mike Haworth, the lieutenant observer in aircraft 4F, sighted *Vittorio Veneto* and reported her position, course, and speed. He arrived in good time to observe 829 Squadron's attack on *Vittorio Veneto* and remained until dusk sending in regular reports.

Following the sighting report earlier in the afternoon by a Royal Air Force Sunderland of an enemy battlefleet, Blenheim bombers had been sent in from Menidi airfield in Greece to attack with bombs.

It may be useful at this stage to refer to Iachino's account and to determine his appreciation of the position and assessment of the forces that were now following him. He seems to have been singularly unworried, except for apprehension over bombing attacks to be expected from shore bases.

"At noon", he says, "I was brought two signals stating that the carrier *Formidable* had sailed from Alexandria and had flown off aircraft to attack us." He concluded, in the absence of further reports, that it was logical to believe that the *Formidable* had only just left harbour and was a long way from them, and that the battlefleet had not sailed at all. Later, at 2.25 p.m., he received two conflicting signals. The first was a much delayed signal from Rhodes which stated that at 12.25 p.m. reconnaissance aircraft had reported one battleship, one carrier, six cruisers, and five destroyers in a position which Iachino estimated to be 80 miles to the east of him. The second, from Naval High Command, based on radio direction-finding cross bearings, reported enemy ships in a position at 1.15 p.m., which Iachino found to be 170 miles to the south-east of him.

His opinion of aircraft reports was that they were unreliable, particularly in regard to reported positions. On the other hand he tended to accept positions obtained from radio direction-finding cross bearings as being accurate. The truth was that it depended very much on circumstances, and in both cases meteorological conditions, instrumental errors, and personal factors could affect the result. Iachino's prejudice, however, led him to a false appreciation. For a correct understanding of subsequent events it is important to read his own words on the deductions he made at this time.

"Positions", he says, "fixed by the intersection of D/F bearings were generally more accurate than those given by aircraft as the latter were greatly influenced by meteorological factors."

Iachino's final appreciation of the situation at 3 p.m., based on the small amount of information received, was that, apart from the four *Orion* cruisers, only a single carrier escorted by a battleship and minor vessels was at sea. This group had inferior speed and was a long way astern. He did not think that it could, or hoped, to close the 170 miles separating them. Iachino still felt that the real danger lay only in British air attacks.

Throughout the battle Iachino seems to have been far more concerned about air attacks on his fleet than from any danger that could result from a gunnery engagement with enemy ships. He knew that his ships were materially superior in both fire power and speed and could therefore choose their own advantageous moment. Air attack could, however, quite apart from achieving material damage, bring about a serious reduction of speed which would immediately neutralise his greatest asset, that of freedom of movement. In particular he knew that the most serious danger in this direction lay in the potential threat of torpedo bombers operated by the Fleet Air Arm. If, however, he maintained a reasonable distance from airfields and carriers the chances of a successful operation by the enemy were small, for his fleet had first to be located, a difficult operation, and then attacked in the face of a withering fire from all his ships.

Iachino describes the noon attack to which the *Trieste* cruisers had been subjected by the three Swordfish carrying torpedoes from Maleme. Sansonetti's ships dispersed rapidly and put up a fierce barrage that forced the planes to drop their torpedoes at a long range. The attack was unsuccessful, but Vice-Admiral Sansonetti of the *Trieste* division thought that he saw one of the planes hit and brought down.

Iachino also refers to the high altitude bombing to which his fleet was subjected by Royal Air Force bombers. (See Appendix III.) *Vittorio Veneto* was attacked by three Blenheims at 2.20 p.m. Bombs were dropped and fell close alongside, between 50 and 150 metres to port and starboard. They threw up great columns of water but caused no damage. Half an hour later six more Blenheims attacked from a high altitude. The same evasive action was taken, and anti-aircraft fire was opened. All the bombs fell into the sea. There were further attacks by Royal Air Force bombers at 3.20 p.m. and 5 p.m. on the *Trieste* group, and, although near misses were claimed, no hits were scored. The *Zara* group of cruisers was "repeatedly attacked by bombers between 3.15 p.m. and 4.45 p.m. without result".

Iachino complains that there was not a single Italian or German aircraft in the sky to defend them at this time. "I felt pretty well deceived", says Iachino "by the lack of cooperation. We continued to remain for the rest of the day without any fighter cover."

Many claims were made on both sides, says Iachino, concerning direct hits, and were supported by statements that smoke and flames had been seen rising from the point of explosion. Although such claims were made in good faith, Iachino believed that they were due in many instances to wishful thinking and illusions which arose in the heat and smoke and noise associated with all attacks. He implies that he would discount most aircraft action reports as being "highly exaggerated".

At 3.19 p.m., Iachino received what he calls the most important attack on *Vittorio Veneto*, "conducted this time with particular ability and bravery in aircraft which had evidently come from an aircraft carrier".

This was the arrival of *Formidable*'s second torpedo strike provided by aircraft of 829 Squadron led by Dalyell-Stead, and which coincided with the high level bombing attack by the Royal Air Force.

"Whilst everyone was busy with the high level bombers", says Iachino, "three torpedo aircraft approached without being sighted until very close."

Dalyell-Stead's squadron had sighted the battleship at 3.10 p.m., following an earlier report from aircraft 4F, and, having worked up into the sun, managed to get down to 5,000 feet before being observed by one of the two destroyers acting as a screen ahead of *Vittorio Veneto*. As the three Albacores, 5F, 5G, 5H, swung round and attacked from ahead, the battleship turned 180° to starboard and splashes were seen on her port bow and amidships. The second sub-flight of two Swordfish 5K and 4B saw the battleship turning, and, deciding to attack her starboard side, immediately dived from 8,000 feet. They saw large splashes on her starboard side and starboard quarter.

Iachino describes the machine-gunning of the bridges and upper works by the fighter escort, which momentarily surprised and paralysed the look-outs and gunners in his own force, and then enabled the three Albacores to continue their head-on attack without being unduly disturbed. An immediate alteration of course was necessary, but before the ship began effectively to turn to starboard an interminable interval of time seemed to pass during which "we all had our hearts in our mouths and our eyes fixed on the aircraft".

The Albacores continued at top speed towards *Vittorio Veneto* without being seriously threatened by gunfire from the pom-poms and machine-guns that had been attacked by the Fulmars. After some time, however, the guns opened up on the new targets. All three aircraft had got close in and dropped their

torpedoes at a relatively short distance. Iachino particularly mentions the aircraft which was leading and which showed very great
skill and courage in approaching so close before dropping. He
saw the torpedo fall in the water little more than 1,000 yards
ahead of the ship just as the ship began to turn slowly to starboard.
He also clearly saw the track of the approaching torpedo. The
next few seconds seemed like hours. Machine-gun fire, however,
now became more intense and accurate and the pilot who had
come in so close was obviously in great difficulty. Fire from every
gun concentrated on him. In a bold manœuvre to escape, he
turned sharply to his left, as if to cross *Veneto*'s course and escape
to her starboard hand where the fire was less intense. At this
moment he presented a full target to the forward machine-guns
which were firing point blank at him. The aircraft received many
hits. Suddenly it staggered, dipped violently across the track a
dozen yards ahead of *Veneto*'s bows, and finally dropped into the
sea about 1,000 yards on the starboard hand.

"And so died a brave pilot without the satisfaction of knowing
that his attack had been successful", wrote Iachino.

So died also Cooke, the observer, whom I had known when
he was a cadet at Dartmouth in the late 'twenties, and Blenkhorn
the P.O. air gunner. A gallant end for three of our brave shipmates.

Every second the torpedo came nearer, with *Veneto* swinging
rapidly to starboard. A hit aft seemed inevitable. A few seconds
after the aircraft had crashed, the torpedo hit *Veneto*; just above
the outer port screw about 15 feet below the water line. The
impact was tremendous. Thousands of tons of water were quickly
shipped. At 3.30 p.m. the engines stopped. Slowly *Vittorio Veneto*
began to list to port. Inch by inch she settled by the stern.

To add something for good measure one of the Royal Air
Force planes at this moment scored a near miss close to the stern:
so close that a great column of dirty water fell on the quarterdeck.
Now perhaps her fate was really sealed.

Sixty-five miles astern of her, still unknown to Iachino, was the
British battlefleet steaming towards her at 22 knots.

Mike Haworth, who was watching it all from aircraft 4F, and making regular reports, writes:

> "The attack was delivered in two waves because the Albacores in the striking force climbed at a higher speed than the Swordfish. Diving out of the sun, the leading sub-flight appeared to achieve a degree of surprise and the enemy made a turn of 180 degrees to avoid." After observing the first sharp turn, Haworth saw "an emission of smoke rings from the funnel, and a further 180 degrees turn to revert to the original retreating course, at which time it was observed that the formation was proceeding at such a speed that the destroyers made no noticeable wake. There can be no denying that enemy speed was very materially reduced."

An hour later 829 Squadron's aircraft returned to *Formidable*. Having taken off soon after noon, they had been airborne for over four hours, and had taken part in one of the most crucial parts of the battle. One by one these gallant men landed on, each unaware of the other's success or fate until they assembled for re-briefing in the operations room. One aircraft was very late: almost at the end of her endurance. Another, however, was missing altogether, and, as the limiting time of endurance was reached and passed, our hopes of Dalyell-Stead's safe return diminished. We could never give up hope altogether, for many was the time when our airmen had had to return to a shore base or had been picked up after ditching.

Three possible hits were claimed and reported by Rear-Admiral (Air), to which the Commander-in-Chief replied "Well done. Give him another nudge at dusk." In the obscuration caused by flash, smoke, and water splash it would be difficult for any to be certain of results, and, while credit generally was rightly given to Dalyell-Stead by the posthumous award of the D.S.O., every member of this small group of five aircraft under his resolute leadership must be regarded as taking a share of responsibility for the successful hit which crippled *Vittorio Veneto*. Lieutenant A. S. Whitworth, the pilot of 5F, and second-in-command, wrote his report for the C.O. of 829 Squadron who failed to return. He says:

"The leader dived to attack about 15.10, and was unobserved to 5,000 feet when the port leading destroyer opened fire. At this moment the two fighters attacked, with the result that this destroyer did a violent turn to port, at the same time as the battleship started to turn to starboard. At this point I dived straight to her outer bow and dropped. The observer and his gunner of aircraft 5H both confirm that shortly after this a column of water arose amidships the port side. After this no definite information regarding this aircraft is available. 5H dropped just after 5G but further to the outer bow. A second column of water under the port quarter was seen by his crew while making their getaway.

"The column of water off the port quarter was seen by nearly all crews. I consider it a hit."

We received encouraging news in a message from Mike Haworth from shadowing aircraft 4F, made at 3.58 p.m.:

"Enemy has made a *large* decrease in speed."

10

Locating the Enemy

PRIDHAM-WIPPELL'S cruisers had joined Cunningham at 12.30 p.m. and taken station ahead of the battlefleet on a bearing of 290° at maximum visual signalling distance. No visual contact of the enemy by surface vessel had been made since *Vittorio Veneto* had broken off action in the late forenoon, and, although aircraft reports continued to flow in throughout the afternoon, there were some differences concerning composition and disposition, and so much uncertainty about the speeds of the enemy, that Cunningham decided that it would be necessary to send on his cruisers at full speed so as to gain visual touch as soon as possible. At 4.44 p.m., therefore, Pridham-Wippell was ordered to press on at full speed, and the destroyers *Nubian* and *Mohawk* were sent on ahead of the battlefleet to act as a visual link between Pridham-Wippell and Cunningham. Two hours of daylight still remained, and if it were true that *Vittorio Veneto* had been really stopped or considerably slowed down, the chances of a decisive engagement before nightfall were quite high. But first to find the quarry.

Orders had also been given for *Formidable* to send in a strong torpedo attack at dusk. We were confident of decisive results from this, for the idea of an approach at dusk was more acceptable to the air crews than the approach in full daylight. Accordingly, six Albacores of 826 Squadron and two Swordfish of 829 Squadron were ranged and armed with torpedoes, and after briefing flew off at 5.35 p.m. under the command of Gerald Saunt with instructions to land ashore at Maleme after the attack. Night landing was not at this time feasible in carriers owing to the dangers of revealing position to the enemy. Although an hour of daylight still remained, there was considerable eagerness. Fifty or sixty miles had to be covered before sighting the enemy, after which the striking force would have to take up station well out of range but within sight of the enemy, and wait for the strategic moment, hoping that they themselves would not be seen, and that they could achieve complete surprise.

In the meantime 815 Squadron at Maleme had been making strenuous efforts to launch a further attack. Two Swordfish were ranged and armed with torpedoes and took off for the dusk attack, piloted by Lieutenant F. M. A. Torrens-Spence and Sub-Lieutenant L. J. Kiggell. At 6.10 p.m. they sighted four ships screened by six destroyers at a distance of twenty-five miles, steering 320° at about 14 knots. Unfortunately they themselves were sighted by the enemy ships, and the element of surprise for the forthcoming dusk attack was at once removed. Half an hour later they saw Saunt's force coming in from the eastward and took station in the rear. It was still light, being about five minutes before sunset.

In *Warspite* the general position still remained far from clear, "due to the presence of both ship-borne and shore-based reconnaissance aircraft, a considerable change of wind, the presence of several separate enemy squadrons, and finally the ever-present difficulty of distinguishing the silhouette of enemy warships". The Commander-in-Chief was now forced, however, to make plans for the night so that his intentions could be made known to his fleet. At 6.10 p.m. he made the following signal:

> "If cruisers gain touch with damaged battleship, 2nd and 14th destroyer flotillas will be sent to attack. If she is not then destroyed, battlefleet will follow in. If not located by cruisers I intend to work round to the north and then west and regain touch in the morning."

The cruisers had been pressing on at full speed for an hour and a half and there was good reason to believe that they would make contact before nightfall, though all depended on the extent to which the Italian fleet had been slowed down by *Formidable*'s afternoon torpedo strike. The British destroyers were organised for the night attack. The 10th Flotilla, consisting of the *Stuart* with D10, Captain H. M. L. Waller, D.S.O., R.A.N., *Griffin*, *Greyhound*, and *Havock*, were to take station ahead of the battlefleet to act as a screen. The 14th flotilla, consisting of the *Jervis* with D14, Captain Philip Mack, D.S.O., *Janus*, *Nubian*, and *Mohawk*, the last two to join at dusk on completion of their duty as visual link with the cruisers, were to take up station one mile on the port bow of the battlefleet. The 2nd Flotilla, consisting of the *Ilex* with D2, Captain H. S. L. Nicholson, D.S.O., *Hasty*, *Hereward*, and *Hotspur*, were to take up station one mile on the starboard bow.

With so many enemy reports being made by aircraft, it might thoughtlessly be assumed that the position should have been clear. It must be realised, however, that accurate observing and reporting depends on considerable experience which requires not only a wide knowledge of warship silhouettes and all the pitfalls pertaining thereto, but a skilful judgment of ship speeds which can only accurately be assessed by a knowledge of the appearance of bow waves, stern wakes, and smoke movements. To the trained and experienced naval observer this is child's play, but to the young newly-joined observers, of which we had many at that time, and who tried to make up in enthusiasm what they lacked in experience, there were endless difficulties, particularly in unforeseen circumstances. Even an experienced and skilful observer such as Mike Haworth, referring to the changes in the disposition of the Italian Fleet, stated that "the close formation that they adopted defied the vocabulary of the Naval Aircraft Code". Good reporting also depended on much more than a good observer. It needed an understanding pilot, good inter-communication in the aircraft, and an experienced telegraphist-air gunner who would ensure that messages were properly sent.

> "The main impression of the afternoon chase", Barnard writes, "was the obscurity of the situation owing to the conflicting air reports". . . . "The plot was most obscure, however, and only a fortunate mistake brought *Warspite*'s aircraft back to *Warspite* instead of going to Suda Bay, as she had been told. The able and experienced observer [Bolt] of this aircraft looked at the chaotic plot while his aircraft was refuelling

and, on being catapulted again, proceeded to make a complete series of enemy reports and amplifying reports exactly according to the perfect observer's 'copy book' and using various signal book groups which we had met in peace exercise, but which we had grown to believe were most unlikely to be used in war. It was a classic example of air reporting, and the many hours and hours spent on observer's training in peace would have been worth it for this one hour alone."

Warspite's second Swordfish carrying Bolt was catapulted at 5.45 p.m. It was less than an hour since he had been hooked on and hoisted on board *Warspite*. It is of interest to read what Bolt writes about this occasion as it helps us to realise how careful preparation and training are pre-requisites of success:

"The staff officer operations [Commander Power] had another task for me and as soon as we were refuelled we were catapulted to clear up the situation caused by conflicting reports about the position, course, speed, composition, and disposition of the enemy fleet. It was known that *Vittorio*'s speed had been reduced, but it was not clear whether another force reported consisted of battleships or 8-inch gun cruisers.

"The last thing I did before take off was to grab three flame floats as I realised that we were going to have to alight at night on the open sea with no organised flare path. We carried out our reconnaissance duties and passed our reports by W/T direct to Alexandria W/T station at a distance of some 400 miles. We had carried out a great deal of practice with this station during dawn anti-submarine patrols from Alexandria and it was very satisfying that P.O. Pace, my telegraphist-air gunner, was able to clear some dozen Operational Immediate messages in a matter of minutes. These signals repeated by Alexandria W/T to Malta and Gibraltar were received immediately in Whitehall W/T and the Admiralty had them nearly as soon as the Commander-in-Chief in *Warspite*."

Bolt sighted *Vittorio Veneto* at 6.20 p.m., and eleven minutes later made the first of his valuable reports. Others soon followed and it became clear that the enemy were still some fifty miles ahead of the British battlefleet, maintaining a speed variously estimated between 12 and 15 knots on a course of 300°. This confirmed the expected reduction of speed, but was nevertheless disappointing as it indicated that a speed was being maintained which could give the British battlefleet an advantage of little more than 7 knots, or, at the most optimistic, 10 knots. To reduce the fifty miles to twelve miles, so as to bring the Italians within gun range, would therefore take at least four hours and possibly more. All seemed to rest now on the torpedo attack by the destroyers which was to follow immediately Pridham-Wippell's cruisers regained visual contact. In the *Formidable* we had high hopes of success from the dusk air attack with torpedoes.

At 6.55 p.m. Bolt reported:

> "Enemy are concentrating. Total enemy force sighted up to time indicated consists of:
> 1 battleship
> 6 cruisers
> 11 destroyers."

This message was soon followed by a further one reporting the disposition of the enemy fleet in five columns, with the battle-ship in the centre column with two destroyers ahead and two astern, and with a column of three cruisers on each immediate flank, and a column of destroyers on the outer flanks. This was even more disappointing, for such a concentration presented a formidable obstacle to any form of attack on the battleship, be it by cruiser, destroyer, or aircraft.

> "By 7.15 p.m. the situation was clear", says Barnard; "the enemy forces had concentrated into one formidable mass and were still proceeding for home on a west-north-westerly course; but they were only some 45 miles from us, and apparently only proceeding about 15 knots. By 7.25 p.m. V.A.L.F. was in radar and visual contact with some of the enemy and a dusk air attack by the *Formidable's* aircraft was due at 7.30 p.m."

Before describing the dusk attack it is helpful to return to Iachino in *Vittorio Veneto*, who had at 3.30 p.m. received a critical blow. As the ship listed to port and went down by the stern the engines stopped completely. Damage control parties, however, were immediately in action. The two starboard engines were started and soon afterwards *Vittorio Veneto* was working up to 16 knots. Iachino states that by 5 p.m. they were doing 19 knots and were able to keep this up. When hit at 3.30 p.m. they were still 420 miles from Taranto, and Iachino complains bitterly at the lack of aircraft, "not a single Italian or German", to defend them. For the rest of the day they were without any fighter cover.

Iachino received a signal from the Naval High Command at 4 p.m. which reported one battleship, four cruisers, and twelve destroyers in a position 170 miles to the south-south-east of *Vittorio Veneto*. Iachino's appreciation when reviewing the position and making plans for the oncoming night, was that the force contained only a single battleship, which at most could do 20 knots and could not therefore catch him before nightfall. He concluded that she must have abandoned the chase, and considered that the real danger lay in the possibility of an air attack before dark, or of a destroyer attack during the night. It was for this reason that he decided on a close screen of cruisers and destroyers round the *Vittorio Veneto*, using his 1st Cruiser Division, *Zara, Fiume* and *Pola*, for the starboard wing, and the 3rd Cruiser Division, *Trieste, Trento* and *Bolzano*, for the port wing. The 8th Cruiser Division, *Abruzzi* and *Garibaldi*, together with the 6th Flotilla, were detached and ordered to return to Brindisi.

Iachino describes with some emotion how he watched these magnificent ships taking up station, particularly those on the starboard wing, little knowing that he was seeing them for the last time. Memories of the past now came to mind. He had served in many of them. There was the *Zara* in which he had served during the Abyssinian war as chief of staff to the flag officer. Then came the *Pola* which had been his flagship until the preceding December. He knew most of the officers; the captain, de Pisa, whom he regarded as a splendid officer, had been his flag captain. Last in the line came the *Fiume*, in which Iachino had hoisted his flag in 1938, when in command of the 1st Cruiser Division. She had taken part in the great naval review at Naples, when these ships in particular had won general admiration for their appearance and fine handling.

While still watching the ships of the 1st Cruiser Division forming up, a quarter of an hour before sunset, Iachino suddenly saw British torpedo aircraft at a great distance astern of the formation.

"These were the planes", says Iachino, "whose job it was to give us the *coup de grâce* at nightfall."

I I

Dusk Strike

ALL DAY Iachino had been aware of the real danger which could
come from the air, but his chief concern was the dire threat not
so much of bombs but of torpedoes. If his speed were reduced,
one of his biggest advantages was lost, and flexibility of manœuvre
denied him.

And now, as the sun sank slowly towards the horizon in an
orange sky on the port bow, he could see eight naval aircraft
flying backwards and forwards in the gathering dusk astern of
him. Eight aircraft hovering like vultures, waiting for the favourable moment when they themselves would be unseen yet could
pounce on the rough outline of their prey silhouetted against the
western sky. At a higher altitude, out of range almost overhead,
Bolt in his Swordfish was reporting every change of disposition,
course, and speed.

> "At sunset", Bolt says, "the Italian Fleet formed itself into a
> compact mass which made it a difficult target for the dusk
> torpedo attack by the Fleet Air Arm. I saw the attack develop
> from a position about 5 miles astern of the Italian Fleet and
> regretted very much that we had had to jettison our two 500-lb.
> bombs before our previous recovery by the ship. The attack was
> most spectacular, the Italian Fleet pouring out vast quantities of
> coloured tracer from their close-range weapons."

All in the Italian Fleet were now at action stations preparing
to open up a barrage of fire as soon as the aircraft approached. It
was also decided that each ship would make smoke, and that ships
on the port and starboard wings would switch on searchlights to
be directed into the eyes of the approaching pilots in an attempt

to provide a blinding barrage. Neither of these devices had been carried out previously in close formation and there was some concern whether they would be effectual.

As the sun went down the orange sky changed to violet, then to grey, through all the colours of a Mediterranean sunset. Darkness slowly descended. Not a solitary light was visible.

At 7.15 p.m., Iachino ordered an alteration of course 30° to port to steer due west. Twilight was rapidly fading, and he hoped that the manœuvre might escape notice or at least upset the plan of attack. Almost at once his rearmost destroyer *Alpino* reported that aircraft were coming in. By 7.30 p.m. the aircraft were very close. It was practically dark now.

Suddenly the tumult began in the rearmost ships. Searchlights floodlit great blankets of smoke; anti-aircraft guns roared out their deafening barrage; machine-guns and pom-poms spat their hosepipe of flame with vicious repetition into the oncoming aircraft; tracer bullets filled the air like fireworks. Gradually the tumult and smoke and fire spread to all the ships encircling *Vittorio Veneto*. Iachino ordered an alteration of 30° to starboard, so as to return to the original course of 300°. As the noise of battle continued, it was impossible to see or hear exactly what was happening. In each ship the fear prevailed that a sudden thud followed by a tremendous shaking of the deck would indicate that a torpedo had found its target.

But let us read a first-hand account from Hopkins, Gerald Saunt's observer in the leading Albacore.

"We set out again towards sunset with the idea of approaching at low level and attacking at dusk. I think we had six or seven aircraft on this occasion and on arrival at the target we found that *Vittorio Veneto* was surrounded by about seven cruisers and a dozen or so destroyers. Whilst waiting for the right light conditions we joined up with two Swordfish which had come out on their own from Crete. At first we thought that they were Italian CR42 bi-plane fighters and spent some time dodging them. When we eventually went into attack from the dark side with the Italians silhouetted against the last glow of light in the west, we found that we had been spotted at long range and were met with an impassable barrage of fire. We were forced to withdraw, and split up and came in again individually from different angles. The barrage of fire put up by the Italians was immensely spectacular but not very effective. A good deal of hose-piping went on which resulted in a number of their ships hitting each other but little damage to our aircraft.

"On withdrawing from this attack we were told by *Formidable* that she could not accept us back on board as she may get involved in a surface action and that we should try to get back to Maleme in Crete if we could.

"Not all of us succeeded in getting there and, in fact, I believe only two or three of us, including myself, arrived at the airfield. The remainder ditched at various points around the shores of Crete but all were picked up or got ashore."

In the *Formidable* we were uncertain of the results of the attack, and this time we were denied the opportunity of first-hand reports from the crews on completion of their attack. Nevertheless we were optimistic. It was now dark and there was no night work appropriate to a carrier at this time. A year at least was to pass before night air operations in a fleet expecting action were developed. Apart from the usual look-out and radar operators who remained on watch most men secured from their action stations. Everybody was tired. The air crews who still remained on board were desperately fatigued after the early start and strenuous day, and turned in early.

Bolt had been relieved of his shadowing at 7.50 p.m., having been told to return to Suda Bay in Crete.

"At this time", says Bolt, "*Formidable* sent a relief aircraft to shadow the Italian Fleet, and we took departure for Suda Bay. The night was clear and moonless and I expected that the alighting on the water without a flare path would present my pilot with some difficulty. Suda Bay was steep too and narrow, and with all shore lights blacked out was not the sort of place to take liberties with on a very dark night. The entrance to the harbour was protected by two booms watched by patrol craft. As the sea was calm I decided we could land outside the harbour and, after doing a low-level run, to put down a line of flame floats, we turned and made a good landing. [This was at 9.25 p.m.] P.O. Rice deserved great credit for this achievement as we were landing towards the shore. It was pitch dark and there was no suspicion of any horizon. Furthermore, as there was a shortage of spares we had surrendered our instrument flying panel to the carrier squadron and the aircraft was fitted only with a primitive turn and bank indicator. We identified ourselves to the patrol vessel on the boom and then proceeded to taxi into harbour—a distance of about 5 miles which seemed interminable. The aldis lamp was most useful as a headlight and eventually we met a motor boat which guided us to a mooring for the night. I went to H.M.S. *York* and reported to Captain Portal and it was on board that ship that I heard reports of our night action.

"*York* had been attacked by explosive motor boats a few days earlier and I shared Captain's Portal's regret that his wine store had been flooded. We had been airborne for more than eight hours and had had an exciting and eventful day. However, we were accustomed to night and dawn flying operations and, though the aircraft was not radar-equipped, the open cockpit of the Swordfish enabled us to do many things which were impossible from an enclosed cockpit. Above all, as a crew, we had been together for more than a year and were able to rely on a competent maintenance team which kept the aircraft serviceable through all difficulties with a minimum of shore support."

Bolt makes it all sound so easy.

In the *Warspite* the Commander-in-Chief intercepted a signal at 7.18 p.m., made by *Orion* three minutes earlier, reporting two unknown vessels right ahead at a distance of 10 miles. Pridham-Wippell had at last regained contact, but the sun had already set and the possibility of a fleet action was now remote. A difficult decision faced Cunningham, who now had a concise report on the Italian fleet ahead of him, based on Bolt's messages. He was aware also that probable hits had been scored in the dusk torpedo attack by *Formidable*'s aircraft. Success was near, though it might elude him altogether with the onset of night. There was also the considerable risk that he may be leading his own fleet into a dangerous position. The situation is best described in Cunningham's own words in *A Sailor's Odyssey*:

"Now came the difficult moment of deciding what to do. I was fairly well convinced that having got so far it would be foolish not to make every effort to complete the *Vittorio Veneto*'s destruction. At the same time it appeared to us that the Italian Admiral must have been fully aware of our position. He had numerous cruisers and destroyers in company, and any British Admiral in his position would not have hesitated to use every

29   The 15-inch guns of H.M.S. "Valiant" firing a broadside. In the background H.M.S. "Barham" and H.M.S. "Warspite"

30 *Rear Admiral P. J. Mack, D.S.O.,*
who was Captain D14 in H.M.S.
"Jervis" at Matapan. Killed in
action, later in the war

31 *Captain H. M. L. Waller, D.S.O.*
and Bar, R.A.N., who was Captain
D10 in H.M.A.S. "Stuart" at
Matapan. Killed in action, later in
the war

destroyer he had, backed up by all his cruisers fitted with torpedo tubes, for attacks upon the pursuing fleet. Some of my staff argued that it would be unwise to charge blindly after the retreating enemy with our three heavy ships, and the *Formidable* also on our hands, to run the risk of ships being crippled, and to find ourselves within easy range of the enemy dive-bombers at daylight. I paid respectful attention to this opinion, and as the discussion happened to coincide with my time for dinner I told them I would have my evening meal and would see how I felt afterwards."

For a first-hand account of the Commander-in-Chief himself at this critical time we must read the comments written by Barnard, the fleet gunnery officer.

"The well-known steely blue look was in ABC's eye, and the staff had no doubt that there was going to be a party. Nevertheless, on paper the compact mass of the enemy fleet looked to the staff a pretty formidable proposition for any form of night attack. I think that ABC had probably made up his mind by about 8 p.m. to send the light forces into attack and to follow up in person with the battlefleet, but he nevertheless, on this occasion, went through the formality of asking the opinion of certain staff officers. Neither the staff officer operations nor the master of the fleet liked the idea much, and said so in their very different ways. The fleet gunnery officer said he was keen to let the guns off, but the battleships hadn't had a night practice for months and there might well be a pot mess with star-shells and searchlights if we got into confused night action. ABC took one look at his supposed helpers and said 'You're a pack of yellow-livered skunks. I'll go and have my supper now and see after supper if my morale isn't higher than yours.' "

It is amusing to compare this comment with ABC's reference to "respectful attention" to staff opinion.

If the 14th and 2nd Destroyer Flotillas were sent off to attack, there would be but four destroyers left with the battlefleet and *Formidable*, to deal with any attack that the Italians might decide to make.

Iachino in *Vittorio Veneto* had seen the fire slacken at 7.45 p.m. as the aircraft attack faded out. Searchlights were switched off and ships ceased making smoke. At this moment *Vittorio Veneto* was able to increase to 19 knots. Course of 300° had been resumed, and all appeared well. *Vittorio Veneto* had emerged unscathed. The Admiral had received no reports of damage from his other ships, and for some time was full of relief for having as he thought survived the dusk attack.

Formidable's aircraft had begun this attack at 7.25 p.m. in formation, but at 3,000 yards they met a tremendous barrage and were forced to withdraw and split up. In the individual and independent attacks which then developed it was impossible to see anything clearly, faced as they were with a blinding search-light barrage and a thick screen of smoke. Most of the pilots thought that they had fired at the battleship, but several observers reported a hit on the middle cruiser on the starboard wing which had been attacked from the starboard side, in the belief that she was the battleship. This was the 8,000-ton cruiser *Pola*. The last of *Formidable*'s aircraft to attack was aircraft 5A piloted by Sub-Lieutenant C. P. C. Williams, who made his attack at 7.45 p.m., flying just above the water and pressing in to close range, through a withering fire from every gun. *Pola* was hit amidships on the starboard side between engine and boiler room at 7.46 p.m. All electrical power failed, three compartments were quickly flooded, and the main engines stopped. As Iachino steamed away with his fleet on his homeward course at 19 knots, he was unaware that *Pola* had pulled out of line and had stopped. The news did not reach him until about half an hour later.

Meanwhile Williams, running short of petrol, returned to Suda Bay and was eventually forced to land in the sea. He selected a good spot near the destroyer *Juno* and with his crew was picked up by one of *Juno*'s boats. His successful hit was to have very important results. But the credit must be shared by all these gallant occupants of the ten aircraft that took part in the attack. Torrens-Spence, the pilot of one of the two Swordfish from Maleme, dived some time after Williams. He says: "We were met by A.A. fire from all directions and were hit in the tail, but got away successfully. No results were observed. I landed at Maleme at 2120."

Saunt reporting the dusk strike says: "The results were difficult to assess in the light conditions prevailing but one hit on a cruiser was observed."

About this time Iachino received a signal from the Naval High Command reporting, from D/F bearings, enemy flagship in a position which he found to be 75 miles astern of *Vittorio Veneto*. Iachino was not alarmed and his reason for this was that no information of a large enemy force had reached him during the whole afternoon. He concluded therefore that the report must refer to the *Orion* squadron or a group of destroyers pursuing him for a night attack.

On receipt of the news that *Pola* had been hit and was stopped, Iachino was greatly upset. At 8.18 p.m. he ordered Vice-Admiral Cattaneo to turn back with the 1st Cruiser Division and to proceed to the assistance of *Pola*. In the light of subsequent events Iachino has described with some care his reasons for this order. A careful explanation was all the more necessary because a signal from Cattaneo crossed his, and suggested sending back only two destroyers to stand by *Pola*. Iachino, however, considered that the situation was one which required the presence of the flag officer who could best assess the state of damage, and how long it would take to effect the necessary repairs, and make decisions. He was convinced that there was a possibility of an attack from light units, either cruisers or destroyers, or even from submarines.

The Italian Commander-in-Chief gave a good deal of thought to Cattaneo's suggestion, but stuck to his original opinion that the 1st Cruiser Division together with the four *Alfieri* destroyers should return to help the *Pola*. He confirmed this by signal at 8.38 p.m., the order to become effective at 9 p.m., and also informed Naval High Command of his instructions to the 1st Cruiser Division, and of his intention to proceed in *Vittorio Veneto* with the 3rd Cruiser Division, the *Trieste* cruisers, to Taranto at 19 knots. Ten minutes later he ordered an alteration of course for the whole formation to 323° which headed them direct for Cape Colonne. This alteration of 23° to the northward just before 9 p.m. together with the unexpected increase of speed to 19 knots after dark frustrated the night search by British cruisers and destroyers.

Shortly after 9 p.m. Iachino watched the two dark silhouettes of *Zara* and *Fiume* as they turned out of line, followed by the four *Alfieri* destroyers in line astern. Cattaneo ordered a course to the south-east and a speed of 16 knots, ignorant that he was steaming towards the oncoming British battlefleet, now little more than fifty miles away; ignorant also that the magic eye of radar in some of the British ships was sweeping the horizon every few seconds.

"It never occurred to me", wrote Iachino, "that we were within a relatively short distance of the entire British force. I thought the British cruisers had decided to turn back leaving only two destroyers to deal with us."

In *Formidable* all was relatively quiet as we steamed to the north-west in line ahead with the Fleet at the maximum speed of the battleships. This was a comfortable speed for us. We were now well to the west of Crete. The nearest point of land was Cape Matapan, eighty miles to the north-east of us. There was no moon, and a haze obliterated the stars. After the racket of the day, the vibration of high speed, the blasts of the assisted take-offs, the roar of aircraft engines, the whirr of the arrester wires, and the general excitement of the various phases of the battle, the quiet on board seemed strangely marked.

"It's ten to one we won't catch 'em now", said the First Lieutenant. And already we were beginning to feel frustrated and despondent. It had been a long and tiring day, and for the loss of one aircraft and three gallant shipmates we had scored some probable hits on the enemy. But as far as we knew they were all legging it for home.

We turned in to get some much needed sleep. Perhaps the dawn would bring further news.

In the radar room the operator kept watch on the radar screen.

12

Night Search for 'Vittorio Veneto'

In *Warspite* the Commander-in-Chief returned to the bridge, having had his supper, and having come to a decision to send the destroyers in to attack and complete the destruction of *Vittorio Veneto*.

> "As soon as he came on deck after supper", says Barnard, "every available sound destroyer was sent ahead to form the attacking force under D14, while the battlefleet prepared to engage the enemy by night, screened by only 4 destroyers (jestingly classified as the old, the halt, the maimed and the blind)."

The details of the scheme had been signalled at 6.10 p.m., and at dusk the 14th Destroyer Flotilla and 2nd Destroyer Flotilla had taken up a preparatory position a mile ahead of the port and starboard bows of the battlefleet, to await the executive signal. This left only the four destroyers of the 10th Destroyer Flotilla to protect the British battlefleet should the Italians decide on a night attack. *Orion* had made contact and reported two unknown vessels bearing 295° distant ten miles at 7.15 p.m., and, with an analysis of Bolt's detailed reports on the plot, the Commander-in-Chief considered that he had at last a complete picture and was ready for a night action. If the damaged battleship was not destroyed by the torpedoes of his destroyers he would follow in with his battleships.

At 8.37 p.m. the Commander-in-Chief made the executive signal as follows:

"IMMEDIATE.
"14th D.F. 2nd D.F. from Commander-in-Chief.

> "Destroyer flotillas attack enemy battlefleet with torpedoes.
> "Estimated bearing and distance of centre of enemy battlefleet
> from Admiral 286° 33 miles at 2030.
> "Enemy course and speed 295° 13 knots."

The eight destroyers under Captain Mack in *Jervis* now drew ahead, increasing to 28 knots and forming in two columns six cables apart, to steer 300°. The first lieutenant of the *Hotspur*, Hugh Hodgkinson, afterwards wrote*:

> "As the executive signal was made, the great arc of the destroyer screen faded and became shapeless as each destroyer foamed up to thirty knots, and turning and twisting like snipe, they fell into single lines astern of their leaders. Then we sped into the westward and the darkness, into fervid anticipation."

Cunningham, in *A Sailor's Odyssey*, writes:

> "My morale was reasonably high when I returned to the bridge, and I ordered the destroyer striking force off to find and attack the enemy. We settled down to a steady pursuit with some doubts in our minds as to how the four destroyers remaining with the battlefleet would deal with the enemy destroyer attacks if the Italians decided to make them. At this stage the enemy fleet was estimated to be 33 miles ahead."

The estimate of 33 miles must have been based on a plotted speed of the enemy of 13 knots: both figures were reported in the executive signal to the destroyers. Bolt's initial estimate of speed had been 13 knots, but he had later stepped this up to 15 knots. We know from Iachino's account that his speed was substantially higher than 13 knots, and from 7.45 p.m. he was in fact steaming at 19 knots. At 8.30 p.m. his distance from the British battlefleet, of whose presence he was still unaware, was fifty-seven miles. (See diagram opposite.) The Commander-in-Chief's signal, therefore, although giving the approximate bearing of the enemy correctly (286°), underestimated the distance by twenty-four miles, and the speed by 6 knots. These discrepancies were to have grave consequences.

Furthermore at 8.48 p.m., as we have seen, Iachino at the time

* *Before the Tide Turned.*

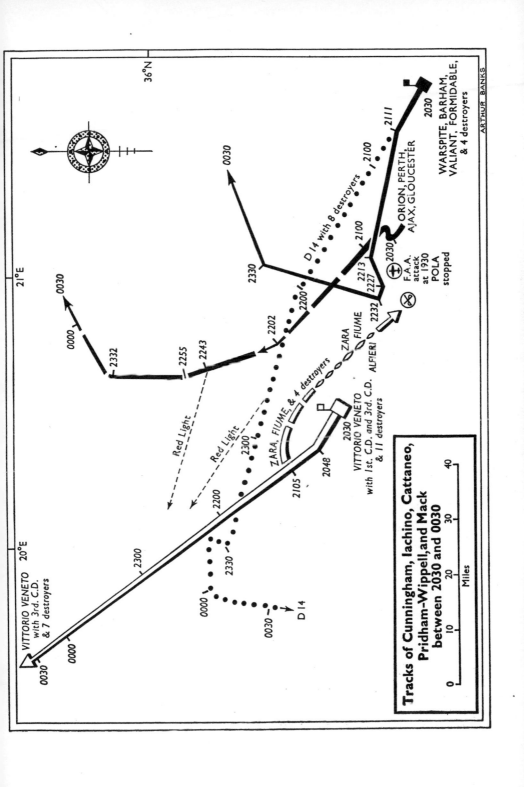

Tracks of Cunningham, Iachino, Cattaneo, Pridham-Wippell, and Mack between 2030 and 0030

ARTHUR BANKS

of detaching his 1st Cruiser Division, altered course from 300° to 323°, so as to head direct for Cape Colonne.

Mack signalled at 9.15 p.m. to the 2nd Destroyer Flotilla and Pridham-Wippell that he intended to pass up the starboard side of the damaged battleship out of visible range, and then to attack from ahead. He would alter from 300° to 285° at 10 p.m. Mack was navigating from his own plot and using the estimates of enemy course, speed, and position as received from the Commander-in-Chief, and was also entirely ignorant of Iachino's alteration to 323°. Mack altered at 10 p.m. and later intercepted a message made by *Ajax,* one of the ships fitted with radar, which reported that at 9.55 p.m. she had on her radar screen "three unknown ships bearing between 190° and 252°, distant five miles from the position 35° 19' North, 21° 15' East."

Mack plotted the reported position of the three unknown ships and found them to be roughly on his course, four miles ahead of his own 9.55 p.m. position. He therefore assumed that the reported ships referred to his own force. Once again on this long day of mistakes on both sides was the error made of assuming one's own force to be the subject of what was, in fact, a report of the enemy. From a subsequent analysis it is clear that Mack passed fairly close to Pridham-Wippell's force, just about the time that the three unknown ships were reported. The three unknown ships were of course Admiral Cattaneo's force returning to the assistance of *Pola*. It is evident that there was a discrepancy between the plotted positions of Pridham-Wippell's force and Mack's force. Cattaneo's force was not four miles ahead of D14 at 9.55 p.m., but about ten miles on his port bow to the south-westward steaming to the south-eastward to rejoin the stopped *Pola*.

Mack continued on his course of 285° until 11.20 p.m., still under the impression that he was passing ahead and to starboard of the Italian battleship which he believed to be steaming 295° at 13 knots, as reported by the Commander-in-Chief at 8.37 p.m. In fact Iachino had passed well ahead of D14 and was almost thirty miles to the northward of him.

Shortly before this, D14 received the Commander-in-Chief's

32   *The cruisers H.M.S. "Orion", H.M.S. "Ajax", H.M.S. "Perth", and H.M.S. "Gloucester" draw the enemy towards the Battlefleet*

From a painting by Rowland Langmaid

33   *Sinking of the Italian cruisers "Fiume" and "Zara" during the night action at Matapan*

From a painting by Rowland Langmaid

34 *S79 retiring after firing torpedo at H.M.S. "Formidable": forenoon of 28th March 1941*

35 *Luftwaffe attack on H.M.S. "Formidable": afternoon of 29th March 1941*

36 *One of several near misses during Luftwaffe attack on H.M.S. "Formidable"*

signal, about which we shall read in the next chapter, ordering all forces not engaged in sinking the enemy to retire north-eastward. Mack turned north-east and asked by signal if the order included his flotilla. At 11.37 p.m. he received the reply "After your attack", and turned at 11.40 p.m. to the westward to resume his attack. After twenty minutes on a westerly course, 270°, he estimated that he was now sufficiently ahead of the Italian battleship to have crossed his track. He altered to 200° and reduced to 20 knots fully expecting in a short while to meet the damaged *Vittorio Veneto*. It was midnight, and the latter was now thirty-three miles to the northward of him, happily steaming for home, while Mack proceeded to the southward. If she could escape Pridham-Wippell's cruisers, which Iachino thought had returned to base, then the *Vittorio Veneto* was now virtually home and dry; for there was little chance of the destroyers finding her now, as they were not fitted with radar, and by daylight she would be well under the protection of Italian shore-based aircraft.

Under the circumstances Mack could have done no better, but Cunningham considered his decision to go to the northward of the Italian battleship "most unfortunate", not only because it "left the southern flank of the enemy open for escape", but because it "cramped the cruiser squadron".

It is of interest to read an account by Commander Walter Scott, who was first lieutenant of the *Jervis* at the time, and therefore has a better idea of Mack's intentions than most people. Mack always emphasised to his flotilla that a destroyer's main objective was the destruction of enemy surface forces, and that since opportunities are seldom presented twice, the flotilla must be at the highest pitch of training and understanding as a unit.

> "At about dusk", Scott says, "Commander-in-Chief detached Captain D14 in *Jervis* with seven other destroyers, to proceed to the westward and sink the Italian battleship which had been damaged earlier by a Fleet Air Arm torpedo attack. *Warspite*'s Walrus had been catapulted earlier, and was in contact with the enemy; a flow of shadowing reports came in.
>
> "Destroyers were spread, speed increased to about 28 knots and course set to intercept. The picture presented by the plot in

Jervis showed the battleship many miles ahead steaming at about 12 knots to the north-westward, flanked by two cruisers about five cables on each beam, and two destroyers a further five cables away on each side. Captain Mack's intention was to work round ahead and then, dividing his force into two divisions, to come down on opposite courses, each division to pass between the battleship and the cruisers, one division passing at a range of 500 yards each side. Thereby it was hoped that the enemy would be thrown into confusion and might fire on its own side. It was a bold plan, and in keeping with the Commander-in-Chief's known views that the nearer you got to the enemy, the better. What the result would have been if contact had been made it is difficult to think, but it certainly would have been a short and very sharp engagement."

Pridham-Wippell's cruisers had been pressing on at 30 knots to the westward most of the evening and endeavouring to gain visual touch with the Italian Fleet, and had seen the *Formidable*'s aircraft at 6.32 p.m. going in for the dusk torpedo attack. At 7.07 p.m., soon after sunset, Pridham-Wippell ordered his ships to spread on a line of bearing 020°, seven miles apart, so as to reduce the chance of missing the enemy in the dark. They were still opening out when *Orion* at 7.15 p.m. reported two unknown vessels bearing 295°, distant ten miles. Pridham-Wippell at once decided to concentrate his four cruisers in readiness for instant action should he be attacked, and ordered his ships to reform in line ahead. At 7.30 p.m. *Formidable*'s aircraft began their attack and this was visible below the horizon some fifteen miles ahead of the cruisers. The flash of many guns, the glow of distant searchlights, the trace of various colours, filled the darkening sky.

"At dusk", Fisher relates, "we saw a lot of ships hull down ahead. *Formidable*'s strike flew past us and attacked them and we were able to see a brilliant Brock's Benefit of tracer."

Pridham-Wippell in his report, says:

"They must have been very gallant men who went through it."

Course was altered to 320° at 7.32 p.m. and maintained until 7.50 p.m. at which time Pridham-Wippell altered to 290° when searchlights and gunfire were seen to the westward. Visibility was now down to four miles and the Italians out of sight. Pridham-

Wippell reduced speed to 20 knots at 7.45 p.m. in order "to reduce bow waves". By a strange coincidence it was at this moment that Iachino was able to increase to 19 knots, though Pridham-Wippell would be unaware of this, and according to latest reports assumed the Italians to be restricted to 13 knots.

At 8.14 p.m., *Orion* altered course to 310° and a minute later got an echo on her radar screen which indicated an unknown ship six miles roughly ahead of her. Speed was reduced to 15 knots and the ranges and bearing of the unknown ship were plotted for the next eighteen minutes. The plot indicated that the ship was stopped, and Pridham-Wippell therefore reported at 8.40 p.m.

"Unknown ship 240° five miles apparently stopped. My position 35° 21' North, 21° 5' East."

His view was that, if this ship was the damaged battleship, he had now "fixed" and reported the position as required, and it was now up to D14 to go in with his destroyers to finish her off. If it was not the battleship, then it was still necessary for him to regain touch.

Pridham-Wippell therefore decided to lead clear of the stopped ship, and to get round to the northward of her so as to continue his search for the remainder of the enemy. After a jog to the north-eastward, he resumed his course to the north-westward at 8.48 p.m., and at 9.19 p.m. increased to 20 knots.

> "The dusk torpedo aircraft attack on the enemy battleship", says Barnard, "had claimed 'probable hits', and when at 9.11 p.m. V.A.L.F. reported an unknown ship stopped five miles to port of him, and gave her a wide berth while he pursued the main body, hopes ran high that this was the enemy battleship which he was leaving for us."

Unfortunately *Jervis* failed to intercept *Orion*'s report, and D14 sped away on his course of 300° at 28 knots, on a track which converged on Pridham-Wippell.

At this moment Pridham-Wippell had been considering spreading his cruisers again to increase the area of search, when he realised that D14 was converging towards his path.

Fisher described the difficulties of using *Orion*'s radar, an early type of ASV (anti-surface vessel). In early 1941, radar, then known as RDF, was still a very scarce and relatively untried equipment. *Formidable*, *Valiant*, and *Ajax* were at that time fitted with modern sets and did not suffer from the limitations to which *Orion* was subjected. Pridham-Wippell was well served by *Ajax* with her radar reports until a communications failure took place, after which he received nothing from *Ajax*, though, being unaware of the failure, he did not realise that *Ajax* was still making radar reports but that these were not reaching him.

> "*Orion* had an early type of A.S.V. radar", writes Fisher, "which, if I remember rightly, you could use by pointing the ship at the target. The only person who could work it was the flag lieutenant. As we came up on the enemy he was in the A.S.V. office calling ranges and bearings to me in the plot, and I pretty soon bowled out that the nearest ship was lying stopped, and told the Admiral. We reduced speed, I think, while we consulted with the Admiral. Tom Bratt (squadron gunnery officer) was in this consultation. Craske is dead and so of course is the flag captain. The gist of this consultation was:
>
> "'That stopped ship may be the battleship. Wonder whether we ought to go in and see? But Philip Mack and his destroyers will be going in to attack just about now and there could well be an all-British battle. The destroyers are better fitted for this sort of night attack than we are. We'd better leave them a clear field.'
>
> "With that we cleared out.
>
> "My recollection is that we were then 4,000 to 8,000 yards from the stopped ship."

It was at 9.55 p.m. that *Ajax* reported seeing three unknown vessels on her radar screen which indicated that they were five miles to the southward of her. It was then that D14 came to the assumption that *Ajax* was reporting him. At the same time, Pridham-Wippell who received these reports before the communication failure, similarly thought that *Ajax* was reporting Mack's attacking destroyer force. He decided to steer still farther to the north to keep clear of them, and at 10.02 p.m. altered to 340°, intending later to alter course and increase speed with the object of intercepting any of the enemy ships that might be on their way to Messina.

At 10.43 p.m. a red pyrotechnic signal was sighted by both *Orion* and *Gloucester* on the port bow, bearing 320°. The general alarm was at once sounded, and cruisers formed single line ahead, altering course to the northward twelve minutes later. There can be little doubt that this light emanated from *Vittorio Veneto* when Iachino was attempting to communicate with Cattaneo in *Zara*. Pridham-Wippell's intentions at this time are not clear. It is possible that he intended spreading his ships once more to resume the search, though feeling that he was somewhat hampered for sea room by Mack's flotillas. *Hasty*, with D14, also saw the red pyrotechnic signal at the same time as *Orion* and *Gloucester,* but on a bearing of 010°. Mack, realising that Pridham-Wippell had seen the light as soon as *Orion,* made the General Alarm Bearing signal, forebore to investigate and continued on his course for the attack.

> "The red light incident", continues Fisher in his note, "must have been after this [the decision to leave the stopped ship to Mack], but I was in the plot and merely plotted it—at least I think I remember doing so. Its significance did not make much impression at the time but it became famous during the wash-up in Alexandria afterwards.
>
> "A little later we saw the blitz of Commander-in-Chief's night action quite clearly somewhere astern."

At 11.32 Pridham-Wippell altered course to 060° having received Commander-in-Chief's signal ordering all forces not actually engaged to withdraw to the north-east.

By such a narrow margin was the *Vittorio Veneto* missed. At this moment, 11.32 p.m., she was thirty-five miles to the west-north-westward of Pridham-Wippell and thirty miles to the north-north-westward of Mack.

In the meantime, almost an hour earlier, great flashes from the big guns of the battlefleet had been seen to the southward. Hugh Hodgkinson described the view from *Hotspur*.

> "On the port quarter a flash showed up over the horizon and a star-shell hovered in the sky. Then another and greater flash. And then to starboard of the first flash a great tower of flame shot up into the air, lighting the whole sea. . . . The battlefleet had evidently walked into something."

13

The Night Action

PRIDHAM-WIPPELL's report of a stopped ship led the Commander-in-Chief and his staff in *Warspite* to believe that *Vittorio Veneto* had been left for the battlefleet to deal with. Barnard describes some of the preparations made in anticipation.

> "ABC decided that he couldn't see satisfactorily for this sort of night action from the Admiral's bridge, and established himself on the *Warspite*'s monkey's island, alongside the flag captain. The *Warspite*'s upper bridge design resulted in considerable congestion, even for a private ship at night action. To add the Commander-in-Chief, chief of staff, staff officer operations, fleet signal officer, and fleet gunnery officer was not easy. The three latter officers were accustomed to improvise, and had taken some precautions with alternative wandering leads and voicepipes so that they could conduct their respective businesses; but by no stretch of imagination could the result be called satisfactory, least of all for the ship's officers of the *Warspite*."

In *Formidable* many of us had turned in soon after 9 p.m.

There was little that would be required of a carrier during this night. It was nearly seventeen hours since Restall had called me prior to dawn action stations. Before turning in, half-dressed, on the bunk in the meteorological office, I had completed the evening weather chart, and with Restall's help worked out the latest state of upper winds. The weather was still fair, but there was a haze which reduced visibility to four or five miles, and which obliterated the stars and accentuated the darkness of the night. The surface wind was light.

On the compass platform Captain Bisset dozed in his chair. The officer of the watch had little now to worry him apart from station keeping. The general feeling on board was one of disappointment. In spite of valiant efforts on the part of the air crews, we now believed that the Italian Fleet had got away and were well on their way home. We were not aware at this time of the report of a stopped ship made by *Ajax* at 8.29 p.m. In line ahead, with ships three cables apart, the Fleet proceeded on its steady course of 300° at a speed now back to 20 knots, *Warspite* leading, followed by *Valiant, Formidable,* and *Barham.* One mile to starboard were the destroyers *Stuart* and *Havock*; a mile to port, the destroyers *Greyhound* and *Griffin.*

I was soon asleep, ignorant, as were the majority, of the approaching action.

I can never be sure of the exact chain of events following a shattering awakening. Whether it was the actual roar of the big guns of the battleships, or the alarm rattler in *Formidable* that I first heard, I cannot be certain. I remember rushing up the ladder to my action station on the compass platform, donning jacket, muffler, steel helmet, anti-flash gear, and trying at the same time to piece things together for the narrative. There were mighty explosions. At each one *Formidable* shuddered violently. On reaching the compass platform, an indescribable scene presented itself. The picture was dazzled by the vivid flashes of 15-inch guns, the bright beams of searchlights, and the orange glow of huge fires that broke out in the ships under fire. The battlefleet had most certainly "walked into something".

Soon we were heeling over and turning fast to starboard as *Formidable* hauled out of line. The desperate and frightening plight of the Italian ships became gradually obscured by the superstructure as we altered course. At speed we withdrew from the terrible spectacle, for a carrier was of little value in a gun action, and a heavy liability. Shortly we saw the battleships do the same, as they swung away from the raging fires and the attacking torpedoes of enemy destroyers.

It was now just after 10.30 p.m.: barely an hour and a half since turning in, but terrible and decisive events had taken place. In a few moments, ships had been practically annihilated. A substantial part of the Italian Fleet, with which we had skirmished all day, was now abruptly faced with its fate.

Immediately on receipt, at 9.11 p.m., of the report from *Ajax* of a stopped ship five miles to the westward of her, Cunningham had altered course to 280°, in succession, ships remaining in line ahead. The unknown ship was barely twenty miles away from him. In less than an hour, at 10.03 p.m., *Valiant's* radar operator detected an echo on the screen, which indicated a stopped ship at eight to nine miles on the port bow, on a bearing of 224°. At 10.10 p.m. the Commander-in-Chief, who was without radar in *Warspite*, received *Valiant's* report that this was a large ship, more than 600 feet in length, now only six miles on the port bow.

> "Our hopes ran high", says Cunningham in *A Sailor's Odyssey*. "This might be the *Vittorio Veneto*. The course of the battle-fleet was altered 40° to port together to close. We were already at action stations with our main armament ready. Our guns were trained on the correct bearing."

Barnard describes the moment:

> "ABC turned the battlefleet together to investigate, handling the fleet from this moment until midnight in the same way that he would have handled a division of destroyers."

The turn together now placed *Warspite, Valiant, Formidable,* and *Barham* on a line of bearing 280°, each ship steering 240°. (See diagram, pp. 136–7.) Such a turn towards was unprecedented in a night action, for the drill had always been for the battlefleet to turn away if there were a possibility of being subjected to a destroyer attack.

The master of the fleet writes:

> It was widely assumed on the bridge that enemy destroyers would be in company with the large enemy ship, and the Commander-in-Chief was recommended a turn away: BLUE FOUR. But he said: 'If that's the enemy we will turn towards and find out what sort they are and how soon we sink them: FOUR BLUE.' It thus occurred that for the first time in a night action either in peace or war a battlefleet turned towards an unknown force of enemy ships.

In expectant readiness, the ships now in quarter line, held on their way, the battleships prepared for instant action, the carrier, now virtually powerless, ready to haul out of line as soon as the moment indicated. At 10.20 p.m. *Valiant* reported the ship bearing 191° 4½ miles. This put the target on the port bow. *Greyhound* and *Griffin* on the port side were therefore ordered to take station to starboard. Scarcely had the order been given, when *Stuart* at 10.23 p.m., on the starboard side of the Fleet, gave the night alarm. Fine on her starboard bow, bearing 250°, in a completely different direction from that of the stopped ship, loomed the massive shapes of darkened ships steaming across the bows of the Fleet, from right to left, at a distance of about two miles. There were two large ships headed by a smaller vessel and followed by three smaller ships. This was Cattaneo's 1st Cruiser Division and 9th Destroyer Flotilla on their way to stand by the damaged *Pola*. The destroyer *Alfieri* led the line. Second in the line was the 8-inch cruiser *Zara*, and third in the line was the 8-inch cruiser *Fiume*. Then came the destroyers *Gioberti*, *Carducci*, and *Oriani*, in that order. With the *Pola* there were seven ships in all, unsuspecting of the presence of the British battlefleet, before the heavy guns of which they were now practically committed. A cruel fate awaited nearly all of them.

Before the night alarm reached the Commander-in-Chief in *Warspite*, his chief of staff also saw the approaching ships. The most thrilling, though the most terrible, moment of the whole day had arrived. It is best described in Cunningham's own words.

> "At 10.25 when he, Commodore Edelsten, the new chief of staff, was searching the horizon of the starboard bow with his glasses, he calmly reported that he saw two large cruisers with a smaller one ahead of them crossing the bows of the battlefleet from starboard to port. I looked through my glasses, and there they were. Commander Power, an ex-submarine officer, and an abnormal expert at recognising the silhouettes of enemy warships at a glance, pronounced them to be two *Zara* class 8-inch gun cruisers with a smaller cruiser ahead.
>
> "Using short-range wireless the battlefleet was turned back into line ahead. With Edelsten and the staff I had gone to the upper bridge, the captain's, where I had a clear all-round view.

I shall never forget the next few minutes. In the dead silence, a silence that could be almost felt, one heard only the voice of the gun control personnel putting the guns on to the new target. One heard the orders repeated in the director tower behind and above the bridge. Looking forward, one saw the turrets swing and steady when the 15-inch guns pointed at the enemy cruisers. Never in the whole of my life have I experienced a more thrilling moment than when I head a calm voice from the director tower—'Director layer sees the target'; sure sign that the guns were ready and that his finger was itching on the trigger. The enemy was at a range of no more than 3,800 yards—point-blank."

The turn back to line ahead put the battlefleet on its original course of 280°, which was almost parallel and opposite to that of the oncoming cruisers, who were now steering 130° and were totally unprepared for action. There was no time to waste. A formidable array of guns waited for the signal. A tumultuous reception from twenty-four 15-inch, twenty 6-inch, and twenty 4·5-inch was ready. Barnard describes the scene.

"All ships (battleships) were receiving *Valiant*'s radar reports of the stopped enemy broad on the port bow, and turrets were trained accordingly. About 10.20 p.m., when the enemy was drawing abaft the beam about three miles away, it appeared to the staff officer on the bridge that the Admiral was going to pass this one by, and so occurred a glorious fluke. The staff officer operations and the fleet gunnery officer saw the turrets creeping round until they were abaft the port beam, and both felt a bit uncomfortable that 'there might be more stuff ahead', especially since intercepted reports from V.A.L.F's force had indicated that some other ships might be dropping back. So, using his authority to make gunnery signals on the G/C wave, the fleet gunnery officer by a most fortunate fluke, made a 'look out bearing' to bring the turrets right ahead, only just in time, before two large enemy cruisers were sighted very fine on the starboard bow. As a result, the interval from first sighting on the bridge to the armament being on and ready was negligible.

"On sighting, the fleet were turned together to 280° in line ahead and to open A arcs, and fire was withheld while the fleet were turning. The port wing destroyer of the battlefleet screen had been told to clear the line of fire and was sped on her way by a curt 'Get to hell out of it'."

As soon as the alteration of course was complete, practically all the big guns were able to bear on the enemy.

Suddenly the *Greyhound*, now drawing ahead, opened her searchlight. A great beam of light fell directly on the *Fiume*, the third ship in the line. The penetrating beam shone not only on the *Fiume*, but beyond and to the left, and in silhouette could be seen another great ship, the *Zara*, second in line, and the destroyer *Alfieri*, on the extreme left, first in the line. The time was 10.27 p.m.

Simultaneously, *Warspite* and *Valiant* opened fire on *Fiume* with 15-inch broadsides. *Warspite* at a range of 2,900 yards, *Valiant* 4,000 yards. *Valiant* also fired her 4·5-inch guns at the same time. *Fiume* quickly burst into vivid flame, from just abaft the bridge to the after turret. The after turret received a direct hit and was blown clean over the side. Within ten seconds of the first broadside, *Warspite* opened fire with her 6-inch armament; she followed with rapid salvoes. Vividly aflame for practically her whole length, the *Fiume* began to list heavily to starboard.

Cunningham writes:

> "One heard the 'ting-ting-ting' of the firing gongs. Then came the great orange flash and the violent shudder as the six big guns (Y turret was not bearing at this moment) were fired simultaneously. At the very same instant the destroyer *Greyhound*, on the screen, switched her searchlight on to one of the enemy cruisers, showing her momentarily up as a silvery-blue shape in the darkness. Our searchlights shone out with the first salvo, and provided full illumination for what was a ghastly sight. Full in the beam I saw our six great projectiles flying through the air. Five out of the six hit a few feet below the level of the cruiser's upper deck and burst with splashes of brilliant flame. The Italians were quite unprepared. Their guns were trained fore and aft. They were helplessly shattered before they could put up any resistance. In the midst of all this there was one milder diversion. Captain Douglas Fisher, the captain of the *Warspite*, was a gunnery officer of note. When he saw the first salvo hit he was heard to say in a voice of wondering surprise:
> "'Good Lord! We've hit her!'"

Barnard in describing the scene says:

> "The events of the next few seconds will not readily be forgotten by those who witnessed them. The *Greyhound*'s searchlight revealed the enemy caught completely by surprise with

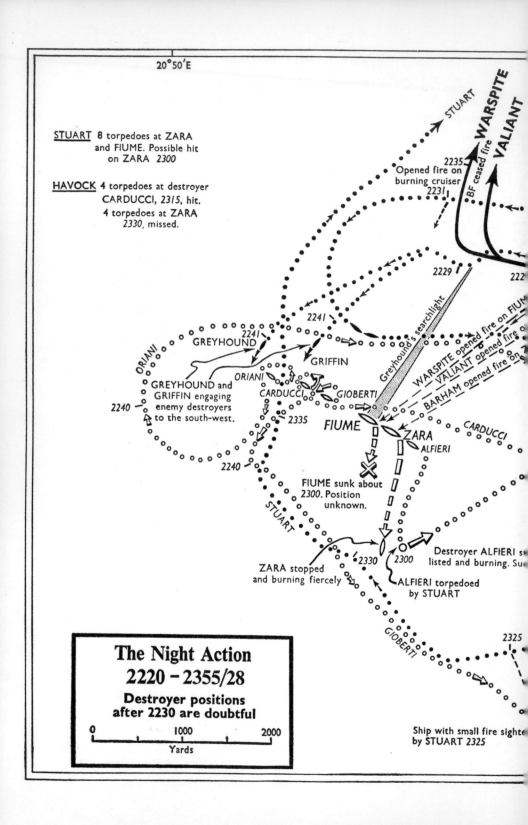

20°50'E

STUART 8 torpedoes at ZARA
and FIUME. Possible hit
on ZARA 2300

HAVOCK 4 torpedoes at destroyer
CARDUCCI, 2315, hit.
4 torpedoes at ZARA
2330, missed.

STUART

WARSPITE

VALIANT

BF ceased fire

2235
Opened fire on
burning cruiser
2231

2229

222

ORIANI

2241
GREYHOUND

2241

GRIFFIN

GREYHOUND and
GRIFFIN engaging
enemy destroyers
to the south-west.

ORIANI

CARDUCCI

GIOBERTI

Greyhound's searchlight

WARSPITE opened fire on FIUM

VALIANT opened fire o

BARHAM opened fire on

2240

FIUME

ZARA

ALFIERI

CARDUCCI

2240

2335

FIUME sunk about
2300. Position
unknown.

STUART

ZARA stopped
and burning fiercely

2330

2300

Destroyer ALFIERI s
listed and burning. Su

ALFIERI torpedoed
by STUART

GIOBERTI

2325

The Night Action
2220 – 2355/28
**Destroyer positions
after 2230 are doubtful**

0   1000   2000
Yards

Ship with small fire sighte
by STUART 2325

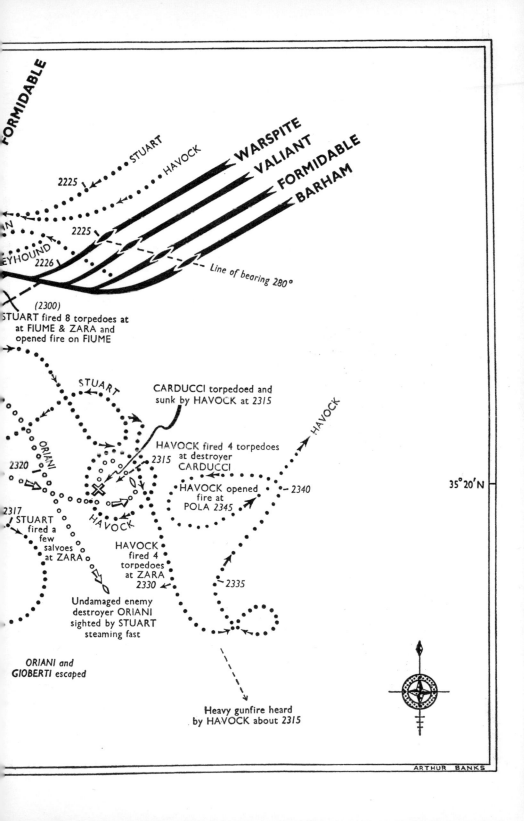

FORMIDABLE

STUART

HAVOCK

WARSPITE
VALIANT
FORMIDABLE
BARHAM

2225

2225

...N

EYHOUND
2226

Line of bearing 280°

✗ (2300)

STUART fired 8 torpedoes at
at FIUME & ZARA and
opened fire on FIUME

STUART

CARDUCCI torpedoed and
sunk by HAVOCK at 2315

HAVOCK

ORIANI

2320

HAVOCK fired 4 torpedoes
at destroyer
CARDUCCI

2315

HAVOCK opened
fire at
POLA 2345

2340

2317

STUART
fired a
few
salvoes
at ZARA

HAVOCK

HAVOCK
fired 4
torpedoes
at ZARA
2330

2335

35°20'N

Undamaged enemy
destroyer ORIANI
sighted by STUART
steaming fast

ORIANI and
GIOBERTI escaped

Heavy gunfire heard
by HAVOCK about 2315

ARTHUR BANKS

their turrets still fore and aft and men running along the upper deck. The *Warspite*'s first salvo was probably one of the most spectacular of the war, five out of six 15-inch shells hitting at intervals along the enemy's length below the upper deck, the right-hand hit apparently lifting most of the Y turret gunhouse over the side. ABC was particularly delighted at the fact that the flag captain, a distinguished former gunnery officer, ejaculated 'Good Lord, we've hit her!' and immediately after the action he ordered this to be recorded in case he should require to pull the legs of Whale Island."

Thirty seconds after her first 15-inch broadside, *Warspite* fired her second broadside into *Fiume*. *Valiant*, having fired her first broadside also at *Fiume*, found that X and Y turrets would not bear on the target. She immediately shifted fire to the left, and engaged the *Zara,* all guns now bearing. With her second broadside, she again scored several hits. In a little over three minutes she poured five 15-inch broadsides into the unfortunate *Zara*, at a rate which astonished even the Commander-in-Chief.

After firing her second 15-inch broadside into *Fiume*, *Warspite* also shifted target left, to engage the *Zara*, the second ship in the line. The range was 3,000 yards. The *Fiume,* listing heavily to starboard, was now a sea of brilliant orange flame. Completely crippled, she limped out of the line, and sank about forty-five minutes later at 11.15 p.m.

Formidable had quickly hauled out of the line to starboard as soon as fire had been opened. This left a gap in the line, with *Barham* bringing up the rear. While approaching in quarter line to port on the course 240°, just before the sudden alteration to line ahead on a course 280°, *Barham* in the rear of the line had seen the stopped *Pola* fire two red lights. These were presumably identification signals to her approaching consorts. *Barham* at once trained her guns on to the *Pola* and was about to illuminate and fire, when ordered to turn back into line ahead. As she was turning, she saw *Greyhound*'s searchlight silhouette the leading enemy ship, the destroyer *Alfieri*. *Barham* immediately trained forward and fired a broadside into her at 3,100 yards. Brilliant orange flashes were seen, and hits were obtained along the whole length of the ship. Thick smoke began to obscure *Alfieri* as, burning fiercely, she turned out of the line, away to starboard.

Barham now shifted to the second ship in the line, the 8-inch cruiser *Zara,* already under fire from *Warspite* and *Valiant.* Six 15-inch broadsides followed, and seven 6-inch salvoes, as *Barham's* contribution.

Zara was now completely crippled and burning fiercely. Her forward 8-inch turret had received a direct hit, as had the bridge and engine room. There were large fires everywhere. Listing to port she continued to heel over in this direction, and as she did so, her bows turned quickly towards the battlefleet. Her starboard side was now presented. Beyond her, making off amidst fierce fires and thick smoke, was the *Alfieri.*

Searchlights continued to illuminate the Italian ships. Early in the battlefleet action, *Griffin,* who suddenly found herself in a most vulnerable position in the line of fire, when *Greyhound* lit up the *Fiume,* had immediately attempted to draw ahead across the line of fire. *Griffin* was soon straddled by a 6-inch salvo from *Warspite.* The commanding officer, now Rear-Admiral John Lee-Barber, C.B., D.S.O., writes:

"I only remember that *Griffin* found herself in the unenviable position of being smack in the line of fire when the 'battle-boats' opened up, and received a very curt 'Get out of the way, you b.f.' from ABC."

No damage was received by *Griffin.* Salvo after salvo poured into the *Zara* now aflame for most of her length. A big explosion took place in one of her boilers, and a forward turret whirled overboard into the sea. Her remaining guns were still fore and aft, for the heavy guns of Italian ships were not fitted for night firing.

At 10.31 p.m., the three destroyers astern of the Italian cruisers were seen to be turning to port to close the battleships, and a minute later one was seen to fire torpedoes. Cunningham at once ordered an emergency turn of the battleships 90° to starboard, and fire was shifted from *Zara* to the destroyers. At this moment, *Havock,* who had failed to switch on her fighting lights, came under fire, and was immediately straddled by *Warspite's* 6-inch salvo.

The Commander-in-Chief saw this display and wrote *Havock* off in his mind as a loss. In fact, *Havock* was undamaged. Barnard writes:

> "The two enemy heavy cruisers were completely crippled by the gunfire of the battlefleet in a few minutes and drew aft on our port quarter, stopped and burning. Then came a somewhat tense moment about 10.30 p.m. when some enemy destroyers, emerging from astern of the cruisers, were apparently attacking us with torpedoes.
>
> "At this time the *Formidable*, which had hauled out of the line to starboard when the battlefleet engaged, was passing up our starboard side and was rather uncomfortably close for the battlefleet turnaway. Handling the fleet as he would a division of destroyers, ABC turned the three battleships 90° to starboard together by fixed light manœuvring signal and shortly afterwards released his four screening destroyers to polish off the enemy. Thus for a time our battlefleet was proceeding 'screened' by the *Formidable* about a mile ahead. Some junior officers felt rather naked at this time, and so I believe did the *Formidable*."

In a few seconds, the battlefleet was heading at speed to the northward. By this time *Formidable* was already three or four miles to the northward of the scene and could see only an orange glow in the sky to the south. Suddenly we found ourselves caught in the dazzling brightness of one of the battlefleet's searchlights, and to our horror the searchlight held us. We felt as though we were naked and suddenly exposed to the menace of all lurking danger. We knew that the Fleet was still on the look-out for *Vittorio Veneto,* and that at night size counts for more than shape when a vessel appears in a searchlight beam. We waited every second for the flash of gunfire.

Cunningham writes:

> "When action was joined *Formidable* hauled out to starboard at full speed, a night battle being no place for a carrier. When she was about 5 miles away she was caught in the beam of *Warspite's* searchlight sweeping on the disengaged side in case further enemy ships were present. We heard the 6-inch control officer of the starboard battery get his guns on to her, and were only just in time to stop him from opening fire."

With heartfelt thanks and relief, we saw the searchlight beam move on, and with somewhat dazzled eyes attempted to re-adapt our vision to the darkness of the night.

The destroyers in company, *Stuart, Havock, Greyhound,* and *Griffin,* were now ordered to finish off the enemy ships. This was at 10.38 p.m. A few minutes later Cunningham received a night alarm signal that had been made by both Mack and Pridham-Wippell now several miles to the north-west, and left him under the impression that our forces were in contact with the remainder of the Italian Fleet. The Commander-in-Chief wished to give the destroyers a free hand in their mopping up operations and also did not want to obstruct any attacks on large or small ships. He therefore made the signal at 11.12 p.m. that all forces not engaged in sinking the enemy should retire north-east, which would enable such ships to withdraw from his battleship on parallel tracks and avoid confusion with those who had work to do.

The signal had unhappy results which are best described in Cunningham's own words:

> "The objects of what I now consider to have been an ill-considered signal were to give our destroyers who were mopping up a free hand to attack any sizeable ship they saw, and to facilitate the assembly of the fleet next morning. The message was qualified by an order to Captain Mack and his 8 destroyers of the striking force, now some twenty miles ahead, not to withdraw until he had attacked. However it had the unfortunate effect of causing Vice-Admiral Pridham-Wippell to cease his efforts to gain touch with the *Vittorio Veneto.*

Brownrigg, the master of the fleet, also refers to the signal, and calls it most unfortunate. He writes:

> "In the general mêlée which ensued, it was clear that our battle-ships were in the way and liable to be torpedoed either by the enemy destroyers or by our own. For that reason I wrote out a signal saying 'all ships not engaged in sinking the enemy 'steer to the north-eastward'. The Commander-in-Chief agreed and we led the battlefleet round to the north-eastward. In the event this was a most unfortunate signal since it led Admiral Pridham-Wippell whose cruisers were shadowing the enemy battleship also to steer to the north-eastward and give up his shadowing task: this had never been envisaged by me or the Commander-in-Chief, since all peace-time training had stressed that in no circumstances should cruisers give up touch."

Barnard in his comment, says:

> "*Formidable* rejoined the line about 11.20 p.m., and the battle-fleet continued unscreened throughout the night. During this period there was star-shell and heavy firing to the south-westward, which it is now clear must have been the Italians engaging each other, and in addition our destroyers appeared to be having a rare field day polishing off the cripples. The Admiral decided to disengage to the north-eastward since there was danger of our own forces engaging each other."

The battlefleet action was over, but the night was yet young.

14

Mopping Up

Six minutes after the emergency turn of 90° to starboard to avoid torpedoes, the battleships resumed course of 280° in line ahead. Two minutes later, destroyers in company were detached to finish off the Italian ships.

The three leading ships in Vice-Admiral Cattaneo's force had received a tumultuous assault. The action had lasted only three minutes. In that time the destroyer *Alfieri* had been blasted by two salvoes from *Barham*. The second in line, the cruiser *Zara*, had received four broadsides from *Warspite*, five from *Valiant*, and five from *Barham*. The third in line, the cruiser *Fiume*, had received two broadsides from *Warspite* and one from *Valiant*. In the middle of an action it is difficult to realise exactly what is going on. The mind tends to focus on one individual scene and event but there are many taking place simultaneously, some connected, others independently, and all are changing with every second. Add to this the element of unexpectedness, and the obscuration by mist and smoke in the darkness, and it may be realised how utterly confusing a night action can be. And throughout is the element of the unknown; the lurking enemy waiting to attack, for which instant retaliation must be ready, and immediate manœuvre decided upon in order to maintain tactical advantage.

Iachino describes how completely paralysed with surprise was Cattaneo's squadron when fired on by the British battlefleet. There was no radar in the Italian ships, which relied on look-outs for warning of the enemy. Action with the main armament was not expected, nor would it have been possible, for there was no anti-flash ammunition provided for the large guns, and problems of gunlaying and fire control at night had not yet been tackled. Iachino also writes with admiration of the precision and speed with which the British searchlights were used, and is also full of praise for the technical efficiency of the star-shell used by the British ships in the action. He refers to the fact that the main armament was not ready to fire in *Fiume* and *Zara,* and an attempt on the spur of the moment, to get them in action somehow or other, failed because the electric power was cut off. Explosion of shells from the heavy guns of the British battleships immediately destroyed all available means of fire control.

After describing the tumult occurring in *Zara,* Iachino states that the admiral, captain, and commander went aft, where a decision was made to abandon ship and to sink her with delayed action charges in the after magazine. The gallant Vice-Admiral Cattaneo, of whom Iachino speaks in affectionate and eulogistic terms, did not survive the action.

To return to the chase. The *Alfieri* had last been seen, almost obscured by smoke, making off in the dark behind the *Zara.* The *Fiume* had limped off to starboard listing heavily and burning furiously. The *Zara* was still moving when last seen, a raging fire, and not under control. Of the remaining ships, the stopped *Pola* had got off without molestation, due to Cattaneo's timely arrival. The destroyers *Gioberti, Carducci,* and *Oriani* had earned themselves a temporary reprieve by their offensive turn towards the battleships and had escaped, as far as was known, without any serious damage. When last seen they had completed their turn to port and steered off to the westward. *Griffin* and *Greyhound* went off in pursuit of these destroyers and steered to the south-west.

"Our subsequent movements", says Lee-Barber, "were unfortunately very dull as we saw nothing until we came upon the *Pola,* stopped and longing to surrender."

A further comment by Lee-Barber is an important reminder of the difficulties, which, in those days, when Britain was virtually alone, hampered so many of Cunningham's efforts. He was always short of destroyers: repair and maintenance facilities were only of a very limited nature. It is with a knowledge of this background that we must read about his various ships dropping out or being unable to maintain the sustained high pace of an action or several actions lasting for some days.

> "As usual ABC had to scrape the bucket for destroyers to go to sea and *Griffin*, having been holed in all the forward oil fuel tanks by a bomb in Malta some days previously, went on the operation with oil fuel only in the after tanks, the forward ones being open to the sea!"

Griffin was not an isolated example of such disabilities, and this point has been covered in Barnard's comments.

> "Before anyone in later years attempts to remark on any aspect of the Battle of Matapan it is suggested that they should first appreciate that the light forces as a whole had been very fully stretched for some time and were always working very near the limit of human and mechanical endurance. The Mediterranean then possessed no escort force. The destroyers carried the whole load and were currently employed escorting convoys to Greece in the face of persistent air attack. The cruisers had been alternating between covering duties in 'bomb alley' and working as high-speed troopships between Alexandria and the Piraeus.
>
> "The destroyer force which accompanied the fleet on this occasion was largely a scratch collection got together by closing up 'boiler cleaners' and deferring essential repairs. As one example, the *Jervis*, the leader detailed for the night attacking force, had only webs of her rudder, the plating having fallen off some time before. She had been going to dock for repairs, but, as was so often necessary in the Eastern Mediterranean at that time, this had been postponed because there was something better to do."

Although *Griffin* found the pursuit "very dull", she and *Greyhound* sighted escaping destroyers, and, opening fire on them, were able to observe hits. The destroyers then turned to the southward, made thick smoke and disappeared. This was at 11.20 p.m.

As *Greyhound* and *Griffin* went off in pursuit of the destroyers at 10.40 p.m., *Stuart* and *Havock* returned to the scene of the action to finish off the Italian cruisers.

It is difficult to render an exact account of the events or the accurate track for each ship, especially as individual accounts do not always tally, and in some cases give a contrary opinion. "They had a wild night", says Cunningham, but he indicates that, although the destroyers did considerable execution, some of the enemy ships reported were ships of their own division. *Stuart*'s account of the next hour is an exciting one. Her track, together with that of *Havock*, is shown on the diagram (pp. 136–7), but these can be no more than approximate owing to the ships' high speed on constantly changing courses, in darkness lit by the pallid light of star-shells, seemingly in all directions, and accompanied by changing vistas from the glow of fires and the flash of gunfire.

Stuart and *Havock* both sighted two ships at 10.59 p.m., one burning and stopped, with another circling slowly round her. It is probable that these were the *Fiume* and the *Zara*. *Stuart* fired all eight torpedoes at both ships and observed a "dim explosion" in the *Zara* which she believed to be a torpedo hit. She then opened fire on the *Fiume*, but, seeing *Zara* move off, followed her and opened fire. A big explosion was seen, followed by large fires by the light of which the ship was confirmed as one of the *Zara* class. Out of the darkness on the port bow a ship suddenly appeared, and *Stuart* had to alter course to port to avoid collision. The ship passed down *Stuart*'s starboard side only 150 yards away and was seen to be a destroyer. This was probably the *Carducci*. *Stuart* fired two salvoes at her, but at this moment caught a glimpse of a cruiser again to the south-west. At 11.17 p.m. she again saw *Zara* and fired several salvoes, having observed the destroyer *Alfieri* which was stopped, heavily listed and burning furiously, suddenly capsize and sink two minutes beforehand.

A few minutes later, while on a southerly course, *Stuart* sighted a destroyer at about 1,000 yards. She appeared to be undamaged, though in fact she had been hit in the forward engine room by a 6-inch shell from *Warspite* when making the torpedo attack on the battlefleet. This had had little effect on her speed. She was steaming very fast on a parallel track. With her high speed she escaped into the darkness. This must have been the *Oriani*, the last destroyer in Cattaneo's line. She was not seen again by the British and managed to get clean away. Before withdrawing to the north-east just before midnight, *Stuart* made a sweep to the westward and northward. During this sweep she reports seeing a ship with a small fire at 11.25 p.m. but again was eluded by the high speed. It is thought that this was the destroyer *Gioberti,* the only other ship of Cattaneo's squadron to escape that night.

Soon after *Stuart* had fired her two salvoes at the *Carducci* at 11.08 p.m. and moved off to the south-west on sighting a cruiser, *Havock* detached herself and attacked *Carducci* with four torpedoes, one of which hit at 11.15 p.m. *Havock* then continued to engage *Carducci* with gunfire, until at 11.30 p.m. *Carducci,* almost awash, and blazing fore and aft, blew up and sank. During this action *Havock* also saw the listed and burning *Alfieri* capsize and sink at 11.15 p.m. *Havock* reports sighting two burning cruisers, one a wreck just about to blow up, and surrounded by a large number of boats, rafts, and survivors in the sea. This must have been the *Fiume,* and the other, probably *Zara,* which had a single fire abreast the bridge. *Havock,* on a southerly course, fired her remaining four torpedoes at *Zara* at 11.30 p.m. but all missed. She therefore retraced her steps steaming to the northward at high speed and engaged the *Zara* with gunfire. It was now 11.45 p.m. Suddenly, in the light of the star-shell fired to illuminate *Zara,* a large ship was seen lying stopped and disabled. Here at last was the *Pola* which had escaped all attention since being hit by a torpedo from one of *Formidable's* aircraft at 7.46 p.m. She had been unable to raise steam on the main engines as she had been hit between engine and boiler rooms. All lights were out and her guns were trained fore and aft. She had fired two red lights at 10.25 p.m., and had had a narrow escape, when *Barham,* who had seen the red lights and trained her guns accordingly, and was about to illuminate her and open fire, had been ordered to alter course at the moment that Cattaneo's division had been sighted.

It was now midnight. *Havock* illuminated *Pola* by searchlight, opened fire at her, and scored two hits. Two fires broke out in *Pola,* one under the bridge, the other aft. To the destroyer this vast cruiser appeared enormous, and the lieutenant in command,

G. R. G. Watkins, at once assumed her to be the Italian battleship which Pridham-Wippell's squadron was seeking in order
to direct Mack's flotilla for the destroyer attack. Watkins now
withdrew to the north-east and at twenty minutes past midnight
reported to Mack and to the Commander-in-Chief by signal that
he was in contact with a ship of the *Littorio* class, "undamaged
and stopped". This was a most dramatic moment. Mack was at
this time some sixty miles to the west-north-westward crossing
as he thought the course of Iachino's fleet. Mack received the
signal half an hour after midnight and at once altered course to
the east-south-east. Watkins sent a corrected report ten minutes
after his original signal, in which he substituted "8-inch cruiser",
for "*Littorio*", gave his own position, and indicated that he was
returning to shadow. This signal unfortunately was not received
by Mack until 1.34 a.m., by which time he had been steaming with
his eight destroyers at high speed for over an hour away from
Iachino. Ironically enough at this moment he was at the position
through which Iachino had passed at 8.48 p.m.: more than five
hours earlier. It was at 8.48 p.m. that Iachino had altered course
23° to starboard for the whole of his formation and headed for
Cape Colonne: an alteration that was not allowed for on any of
the plots of the British ships: an alteration which undoubtedly
enabled *Vittorio Veneto,* and those ships that still remained with
Iachino, to evade Mack's flotillas.

Now, at 1.34 a.m., Iachino was eighty-five miles from Mack
steaming at 19 knots. With his full speed of 36 knots, giving him
a superiority of 17 knots, Mack would have taken at least five
hours to catch Iachino, even if he had known exactly where
Iachino was.

Mack, having come so far to the eastward to look for the battleship earlier reported by *Havock,* decided to hold on. Cunningham
in his despatch was charitable towards *Havock* though bitterly
disappointed that *Vittorio Veneto* had been allowed to escape.
Havock had already sunk the *Carducci* and had found the *Pola.*

"The mistake in *Havock's* signal", said the Commander-in-
Chief, "did not actually bring about any ill effect since the

flotillas had by then missed the *Vittorio* and did useful work in polishing off the damaged cruiser."

Mack in the *Jervis,* accompanied by *Nubian, Mohawk, Janus, Ilex, Hasty, Hereward,* and *Hotspur,* arrived at the scene of the battleship action soon after 2 a.m. The sea seemed to be full of boats, rafts, and swimming men. Course was steered for the glow of a fire on the horizon, and as the flotilla approached it was seen that the fire emanated amidships from a stopped Italian cruiser. This was the *Zara,* still afloat, though abandoned; she had a few small fires burning on the upper deck. Mack ordered rear destroyers to pick up survivors, and made a signal that only *Jervis* was to fire torpedoes. He well knew the risk to his own ships which could happen after formation was broken.

"Closing to 1,000 yards", writes Scott, "*Jervis* fired five. Three appeared to hit."

A tremendous explosion followed; first a great gusher of black water, then a huge fire which spread over the desolate scene for miles, lighting up the wreckage, the boats, and the swimming men. The growing and the rising smoke made her look gigantic, but slowly she turned over and sank beneath the sea. The time was 2.40 a.m. Destroyers were still steaming slowly through the wreckage, picking up survivors on their scrambling nets; no boats were lowered.

Meanwhile in a position about two miles to the east was the *Pola. Greyhound* and *Griffin* had rushed to the scene in response to *Havock*'s signal, and arrived at 1.40 a.m. to shine a searchlight on her and find her with her guns fore and aft, ensign flying, with a thoroughly demoralised party of men on the upper deck, many of whom were half drunk. The quarter-deck was littered with clothing, personal belongings, and bottles.

We were told in the *Formidable* the next morning that, on being asked why their guns remained fore and aft, the reply was given that this was to avoid provoking any retaliation. This agrees with Lee-Barber's remark that they were "longing to surrender". It is possible, however, that the failure of electricity was responsible. The question now was whether to sink the *Pola,* or to board and capture. There was not likely to be much opposition from the crew, but, if *Pola* were to be sunk, the disposal and accommodation of prisoners would present quite a problem. *Havock* on returning to the scene, and having already expended all torpedoes, asked D2 at 3.14 a.m. whether to "board or blow off her stern with depth-charges". D2 replied with a curt "Get clear".

Having sunk the *Zara,* Mack saw recognition signals at 2.50 a.m. two miles away to the eastward. Rescue work was stopped and Mack proceeded in this direction, making the following signal at 3.11 a.m.:

> "C. in C. (R.) V.A.L.F. from D14. Have sunk *Zara.* Am about to sink *Pola.* Large amount of survivors which I shall be unable to pick up."

At 3.25 a.m. Mack went alongside *Pola* and took off the ship's company who still remained. Many had jumped, and some were still jumping overboard as he went alongside.

Destroyers were ordered to pick up survivors. At 3.40 a.m. *Jervis* cast off, made an offing, and fired one torpedo into *Pola.* This hit, but appeared to have little immediate effect. *Nubian* was ordered to fire another. This also hit and at 4.03 a.m. *Pola* blew up and sank.

Scott's description of the scene from the *Jervis* is particularly vivid:

> "Just as the blast of the *Zara* explosions subsided, the flotilla gunnery officer remarked to Captain (D) 'Don't look behind you sir,—but there's another whopper.' All eyes turned to the port quarter and another cruiser (the *Pola*) was seen. She appeared to be undamaged, and lay wallowing in a slight swell. After circling round, Captain Mack suddenly said 'I am going alongside—tell the first lieutenant to fall out the guns' crews, except the pom-pom, and prepare wires and fenders starboard side.' I received this order whilst aft, and sent for the chief bosun's mate who, emerging from the director, received the orders with incredulity, but quickly got things organised. 'A' gun's crew, scenting fun, armed themselves with cutlasses kept for such an occasion in the fo'c'sle locker, and prepared to capture by boarding.
>
> "A perfect approach, and over went a heaving line thrown by the captain of the fo'c'sle and accompanied by the cry 'Take

this, you b-gg-rs'. Take it they did, and our wires were hauled in with alacrity and the ship secured alongside. Uttering blood-curdling cries, 'A' gun's crew swarmed on board the *Pola*. Only 257 of a ship's company of 1,000 remained, and they were hud-dled, cowed, on the fo'c'sle—the remainder had jumped over-board some time previously, shortly after the ship had been hit in the boiler room by a Fleet Air Arm torpedo.

"The 257 Italian ratings filed on board in an orderly fashion over a brow hastily put out, and were followed by the com-mander and captain of the *Pola*. Meanwhile *Jervis*' gunner's party had crossed the other way with a few tools, to remove small arms and, in particular, 20 mm Breda guns, with which we were ill supplied. The task proved beyond them in the limited time, but they came back with a story of chaos on board. The officers' cabins had been looted by the ship's company of the *Pola*, and empty Chianti bottles lay everywhere. Verification of this came when a number of the prisoners showed unmistakable signs of inebriation.

"At last, after about twenty minutes I suppose, I was able to report to Captain (D) that everybody was on board, wires re-rove for slipping, and the ship ready to proceed. Casting off, *Jervis* steamed slowly round and illuminated the dead cruiser with her searchlight. Considering that *Jervis* had had more than her fair share of the fun, Captain (D) ordered *Nubian* to finish off the enemy with a torpedo, after toying with the idea of towing the cruiser back to Alexandria, some 500 miles or so. He reluctantly dismissed it owing to the certainty of heavy air attack next day."

Nubian closed in to 1,000 yards, and fired one torpedo which hit but, to speed the end, fired another which produced the desired result. This was the end of the *Pola*. Of Cattaneo's 1st cruiser division and the 9th destroyer flotilla, only the *Gioberti* and *Oriani* had escaped. *Fiume, Zara, Pola, Alfieri* and *Carducci* had on this momentous night sunk beneath the darkened waters of the Mediterranean sea. With them had perished 2,400 Italian seamen and officers, including Vice-Admiral Cattaneo.

Mack now re-formed all the destroyers and proceeded on a course of 055° at 20 knots to rejoin the flag at the rendezvous appointed for 7 a.m.

"Time was getting on," concludes Scott, "the dawn was ap-proaching, and the battlefleet was still very thinly screened.

> Collecting his flock, Captain (D) set course to join the Commander-in-Chief with an extra load of 257 Italians. Contact was made shortly after dawn, and the Commander-in-Chief again had his brood around him and his battleships safely screened."

In his report on rating prisoners Mack said that they were "a sorry crowd: poor physique: probably the non-swimmers of *Pola*". He went on to tell an amusing story.

> One of the few who spoke English got his own back nicely on an English stoker who was unaware of the fact. The latter came into the mess, and seeing a dejected row of bodies on a stool addressed them patronisingly and loudly in language which, he thought, they wouldn't understand:
> "I bet you're sorry you blokes ever joined that b——y lot."
> To his utter astonishment one of the bodies piped up:
> "You're telling me."

There had been a brisk flow of signals during the mopping-up period. One of these referred to the Italian prisoners.

"Prisoners when asked why they had failed to fire at us replied that they thought if they did we would fire back."

Another was made in reply to C.-in-C.'s query about the number of wounded prisoners on board:

"State of prisoners: six cot cases: fifty slightly injured: one senior officer has piles."

To which the Commander-in-Chief quickly replied:

"I am NOT surprised."

Perhaps it is this exercise of a little humour that keeps us sane on such momentous and tragic occasions.

15

Retaliation

IT WAS now the 29th March 1941. Restall called me at 2.30 a.m. with the usual "Balloon's ready Sir", and "Not a bad morning neither", and added "I reckon we give them Eye-ties somethin' to think about last night."

Formidable was to fly off a dawn search at 4.30 a.m. A forecast of wind, weather, sea, and the upper winds would be required. It was a fine morning with only light breezes and the forecast was favourable.

We were now in company with the battlefleet, steaming to the north-east. Our position was about thirty miles off Cape Matapan and 100 miles from the scene of the night action. Iachino, although we did not know this, was 180 miles from us.

At 4.30 a.m. *Formidable* turned into wind, and we flew off three Albacores to carry out a search in a sector between 160° and 305°. They would be away for a good four hours and in any case we were not now hopeful of any sightings. Another aircraft was sent off to search the area to the west of Crete and then to land at Maleme with orders for our aircraft that had returned there after the dusk strike on the previous evening.

By 7 a.m. all units of the Fleet had rejoined the flag. At 7.03 a.m. C.-in-C. made to V.A.L.F.: "Come under the umbrella." No casualties or damage had been suffered during the night. "As daylight came on March 29th" [writes Cunningham],

> "our cruisers and destroyers were in sight making for the rendezvous with the battlefleet. Feeling very certain in our minds that the *Warspite* had sunk a destroyer in the mêlée the

night before, we eagerly counted them. To our inexpressible relief all twelve destroyers were present. My heart was glad again."

It was *Hasty*, however, and not *Havock*, who "carried the can". At 7.33 a.m. C.-in-C. had flashed to *Hasty*: "You got a couple of salvoes from *Warspite* which should 'larn' you to put your fighting lights on." To which *Hasty* flashed back: "I think I am being confused with another destroyer. I was in company with D2 all last night and no salvo fell near me."

At 8 a.m. course was shaped to search the scene of the night action, reports of sightings of rafts and survivors having come in by then. Soon we arrived in the area. The sea was covered with a film of oil. Wreckage and clusters of men in boats and on rafts extended over a vast area farther than the eye could see. There were many floating corpses. The morning was fine, the sea smooth, and a fatalistic, passive sort of disposition seemed already to have settled on survivors. Our destroyers were detailed to carry out the rescue work. This was a work of mercy carried out in spite of lurking danger from aircraft and submarines. Over 900 men were rescued in a period lasting a little over an hour.

A German aircraft suddenly appeared. The whole British Fleet was in waters within easy reach of enemy shore-based bombers which could quickly mount a heavy air attack. The Commander-in-Chief was compelled to end this work of mercy, so rudely interrupted. The dawn air search had found nothing, so the whole Fleet now shaped course for Alexandria, still a day and a half's steaming away. As we drew away, an aircraft was flown off *Formidable* with a message to be taken to Suda Bay for transmission by radio to Malta, where it was to be broadcast to the Chief of the Italian Naval Staff. This message gave the position of the remaining two or three hundred still in the water. They were rescued two days later by the Italian hospital ship *Gradisca*; she picked up 13 officers and 147 men.

Barnard writes:

At daylight next day ship after ship appeared in sight reporting "No damage, no casualties" until the tally was completed. The reassembly of the whole fleet entirely undamaged seemed to us at the time rather miraculous after such a busy night. Sweeping through the area of the night action was also a memorable sight with survivors' rafts spread over a wide area stretching beyond both wings of the screen. Bombing by German aircraft started very soon after destroyers had commenced picking up survivors, and the fleet had to clear out. ABC showed once again the knightly and very human heart under his iron exterior by flying off an aircraft to make a signal (when at a suitable distance from the fleet) to the Italian Chief of the Naval Staff giving the position where we had to leave the survivors.

Greek destroyers picked up some 110 survivors on the night of the 29th March. This Greek flotilla was unable to take part in the battle through an unfortunate ciphering error in a signal in which the word "orders", was received as "oilers", by the Commander-in-Chief. The signal stated that "seven Greek destroyers" were "proceeding at once through the Corinth Canal to await orders between Cephalonia and Zante". Because of the error, orders were never sent and an opportunity was missed of using this force to assist in the task of intercepting the retreating enemy. In the event, with the reigning difficulty in communications and confusion in reports which so typified this battle, their presence might have added to the difficulties pertaining to local appreciation of the situation.

We knew that the Fleet had been sighted and reported by the German aircraft during the forenoon, and expected retaliation in strength within a few hours. Noon came without any attacks developing. But the weather was fine and visibility extreme. When the attack did come we knew that it would almost certainly concentrate on *Formidable*.

The warning came suddenly at 3.11 p.m. when many of us were making up for lost sleep. On the radar screen a heavy force of attacking aircraft could be seen approaching. First reports indicated a large formation, distant seventy-six miles, approaching rapidly from the north-west. Not a second was to be lost. Within three minutes three Fulmars were boosted from the assisted take-off position at the forward end of the flight deck. There was no time to turn into wind. Even now it would take too long for the fighters to gain sufficient height before the attack developed.

Once again we were caught, for our fighter section which was already in the air had been sent off to intercept two distant enemy aircraft which, it was now apparent, were mere decoys to distract attention from the main formation. The Fleet now went to action stations and all ships were ordered to prepare an umbrella barrage over *Formidable*. Once again the ladders rang out as men in heavy boots and steel helmets doubled to their positions.

Fighters: when and how many? This was always a difficult problem to solve, especially when there was a shortage. If you were too late to allow the fighters to gain height, the attack would develop practically unopposed. If you committed the fighters too early then the attack might be delayed until an appropriate moment presented itself when the fighters had spent their effort.

After fifteen minutes the attacking bombers were reported to be at forty miles. After a further five minutes they were only twenty-five miles away. In three more minutes every gun in the Fleet opened the barrage. The din was deafening. The sky was covered with white puffs and brown blobs of smoke. Jagged bits of steel rained into the sea all around us; it looked like a heavy hailstorm. Now we were steaming at full speed.

Suddenly we saw them. The sun and the smoke bursts almost blinded our view of their approach. They were already in a vertical dive through the devastating barrage. Faster. Nearer. The blast of gunfire was gratifying music. One of the JUs exploded. It caused no more than another puff of smoke.

"Hard-a-starboard", yelled the captain.

We heeled violently over, and began to turn. The first of the bombers was flattening out. The second followed.

"Hard-a-port", yelled the captain.

Again we heeled over violently. A mountain of filthy black water shot up to eighty feet: close to us, but a little away to port. Another followed: much nearer, but to starboard this time. Now a very close one: ahead. Another very close one: on the bow. We watched them all with grim fascination, waiting for the one which must find its mark. The cascades turned to white and glistened brightly in the sunshine. There were more to come; and still more. The later ones fell farther away. In a few seconds it was over and we breathed again. The gunfire slackened. We experienced a feeling of exhilaration and stimulation. There had been twelve Junkers 88 altogether, and the attack, which had lasted only a few seconds, seemed like eternity. There had been four very near misses, but no damage. One JU88 had disintegrated. Another had been shot down. We saw him, slowly it seemed, through the burst of grey smoke, come lower and lower, until with a great white splash he crashed into the sea to port, and instantly disappeared. The bombing from the first six had been alarmingly accurate. The last four of the formation, however, had been forced to drop their bombs hurriedly when attacked by *Formidable*'s fighters.

There were no further attacks this day, but while we were landing our fighters after the attack, the engine of one of the Fulmars cut out. The aircraft crashed into the sea astern of *Formidable*. The occupants fortunately wriggled free and within minutes were picked up by *Hasty* coming up astern of us. Apart from superficial cuts they were unhurt. Joyfully we sped on our way to Alexandria at 20 knots. By nightfall we estimated that we should be free from further aircraft attack. There was the immediate cover of the night, and by daylight we should be only 240 miles from Alexandria.

The next day, 30th March, was Passion Sunday which we spent in sober thanksgiving. We continued our way through the lovely Mediterranean waters, mindful of the great success that had been bestowed on our cause: a timely victory that had not only reduced our nearest enemy by three fast 10,000 ton 8-inch cruisers, which had been a constant threat to our slower 6-inch cruisers and all our smaller and more lightly armed ships whose number were already too restricted, but had paralysed all further military enterprise on the part of the Italian Navy, for they never appeared again for a Fleet action.

Church services were held on board throughout the Fleet on this lovely morning and thanks were given to Almighty God for our victory and for our preservation through the battle. There were many of us who attended Communion before breakfast in *Formidable*'s delightful chapel: a small compartment panelled in light oak, furnished with rich hangings and thick blue carpets. Our jubilation was tempered by the thought of the terrible events of the night action: of the anguish suffered by our enemy: of the widows and the children who would be fatherless: and of our gallant shipmates Dalyell-Stead, Cooke, and Blenkhorn, who had perished, but who had done so much to bring about the victory. We joined with the Reverend Jack Holland, the chaplain of the *Formidable*, in a prayer for victory in this war and for ultimate peace.

Jack Holland wrote the following note about the night action:

> "I can remember standing on the edge of the flightdeck in much the same way as one stands on the touchline watching a rather one-sided game, knowing that this was what we had been waiting for and yet with a queer feeling of pity. There was an Italian cruiser blazing like a torch, stopped and helpless, left behind to sink; we could see the Italians abandoning ship in the light of the flames as we passed about 2 miles away. All the time *Formidable* steamed along silently while the battleships continued firing. A sailor standing near me in the darkness: 'Poor devils, they never had a chance.' All round me the same feelings; a strange mixture of elation, triumph and pity.
>
> "The next day, as we steamed back in daylight past the rafts and debris of the battle, leaving the Italians still in the water knowing that we dare not stop to pick them up, there was this same feeling that we had been spectators and not participants in what may quite likely prove to be the last night action between opposing fleets."

There were further alarms during the day, and *Formidable*'s fighters shot down a JU88.

A submarine contact during the afternoon caused instant action by our destroyer screen.

> "Just as we were approaching the Great Pass into Alexandria Harbour", says Barnard, "a submarine contact was reported right ahead. As there was no sea room to manœuvre, ABC ordered the destroyers to 'clear the area ahead of the Fleet with depth charges'—a spectacular end to an eventful three days."

The resounding explosions of depth-charges quickly reminded us that dangers still lurked in the sea. The Italian prisoners in many ships were horrified at the prospect of renewed action, but nevertheless cheered. The explosions ceased, and the Fleet proceeded on its way. At 5.30 p.m. on this lovely spring evening we arrived at Alexandria and secured to our berth in the harbour. The long-term prospect might look dismal, for we were still fighting virtually alone, but the present was rosy and we had a great naval victory to celebrate.

16

Reflection

His Majesty King George VI sent the following message to the Commander-in-Chief, Mediterranean Fleet, on the 1st April, 1941:

"My heartiest congratulations to all ranks and ratings under your command on your great victory."

This gracious message was received with great joy and satisfaction throughout the Fleet.

The Commander-in-Chief had already made a signal to the Fleet, in which he gave praise to all departments for their contribution to the victory. There was, however, in spite of the satisfaction of a timely victory, widespread disappointment at the escape of the damaged *Vittorio Veneto* and this must have been felt particularly by Cunningham himself as well as by every member of the Fleet.

Cunningham blamed no one and put the matter succinctly in the following words:

> "Looking back I am conscious of several things which might
> have been done better. However, calm reflection in an armchair
> in the full knowledge of what actually happened is a very different
> matter from conducting an operation from the bridge of a ship
> at night in the presence of the enemy. Instant and momentous
> decisions have to be made in a matter of seconds. With fast mov-
> ing ships at close quarters and the roar of heavy gunfire, clear
> thinking is not easy. In no other circumstances than in a night
> action at sea does the fog of war so completely descend to blind
> one to a true realisation of what is happening."

It is clear that the Commander-in-Chief questions the wisdom of his signal made just after 11 p.m. in which all forces not engaged in sinking the enemy were ordered to withdraw to the north-eastward. At that moment the scene of burning ships and the flash of gunfire in various directions was most confusing, and, following the torpedo attack by the Italian destroyers half an hour earlier, it became essential to extricate the battlefleet on a withdrawal course which would be known to all the British ships and which would help to distinguish friend from foe, on this very dark night. Cunningham's criticism of what he calls his ill-considered signal has already been given in Chapter 13. Instead of leaving the field clear for the destroyers to mop up and for Pridham-Wippell and Mack to continue their pursuit of the damaged *Vittorio Veneto,* the signal virtually put an end to further efforts to gain touch. It is, however, only fair to accept the fact at the same time that without such a signal, the battlefleet and *Formidable* could have been placed in great jeopardy in the darkness. A torpedo hit on any of them would have reduced speed and made the victim a sitting target for the German dive bombers who would be within easy reach the next morning.

Had Mack decided to attack *Vittorio Veneto* and escorts from astern, rather than from ahead, his chances of gaining contact would have been decidedly greater. But even with his ahead attack, if only Iachino had not altered course at 8.48 p.m. his chances of contact would have been high. There is therefore little point in discussing such hypotheses. A more important factor concerning Mack's decision to attack from the northern flank of the enemy was that he tended to cramp the movements of Pridham-Wippell's cruisers whose task it was to gain visual contact with *Vittorio Veneto.*

In his despatch Cunningham says:

> "The Vice-Admiral Light Forces was also faced with difficult decisions. As dusk fell he was drawing up on the enemy with his cruisers spread to maintain contact. In the last of the after-glow it appeared that an enemy squadron was turning back towards him which obliged him to concentrate his force. This was undoubtedly a right decision, but from then onwards every time he wished to spread his cruisers to resume the search he was

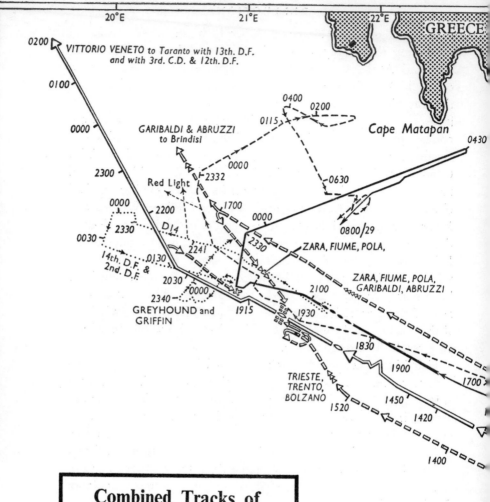

**Combined Tracks of
British and Italian Fleets
28th.–29th. March, 1941**

0   10   20   30   40   50

Mean Scale – Nautical Miles

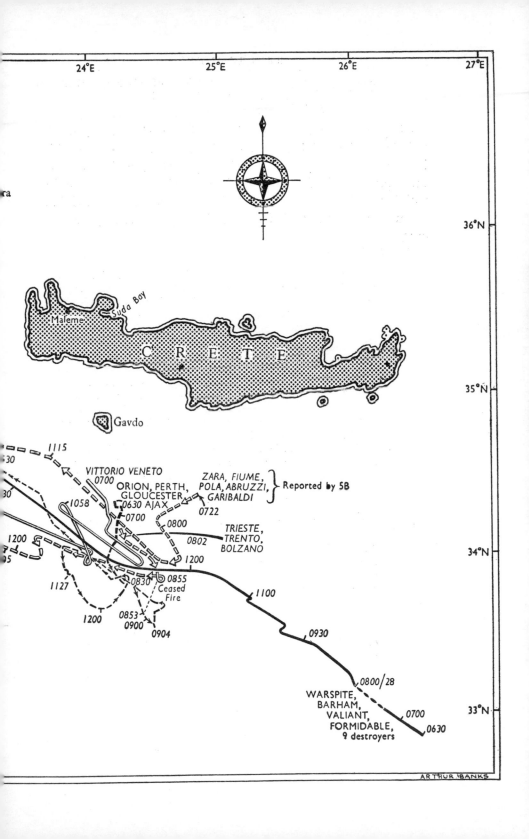

24°E 25°E 26°E 27°E

36°N

Suda Bay
Maleme

C R E T E

35°N

Gavdo

1115
30
30
1058

VITTORIO VENETO
0700

ZARA, FIUME,
POLA, ABRUZZI, } Reported by 5B
GARIBALDI

ORION, PERTH,
GLOUCESTER,
AJAX
0630
0700

0722

0800
0802

TRIESTE,
TRENTO,
BOLZANO

34°N

1200
35
1127
1200

1200

0830
0855
*Ceased
Fire*

0853
0900
0904

1100

0930

0800/28

WARSPITE,
BARHAM,
VALIANT,
FORMIDABLE,
9 destroyers

0700
0630

33°N

ARTHUR BANKS

foiled by some circumstance, not least of which was D14's decision to lead the destroyer flotillas round the northern flank of the enemy before attacking."

Disappointment was all the keener inasmuch as a red pyrotechnic signal was sighted by the cruisers *Orion* and *Gloucester* with Pridham-Wippell, and by the destroyer *Hasty* with Mack, at 10.42 p.m. just half an hour before the Commander-in-Chief's withdrawal signal was made. Admiral Iachino has confirmed that this was made by *Vittorio Veneto* during repeated attempts to get in touch with *Zara*.

Cunningham says:

"The withdrawal order was intended to ensure withdrawal on parallel tracks clear of the destroyer mêlée and was made under the impression that cruisers and striking force were in contact with the enemy. Heavy fighting had been observed to the south-westward which supported this belief. Unfortunately the cruisers were not in fact engaged and the Vice-Admiral Light Forces accordingly withdrew to the north-east. He had sighted a red pyrotechnic signal some distance to the north-west 30 minutes earlier and was at this time about to spread to investigate. This red light signal was sighted bearing 010°, simultaneously by D14 who, seeing it in the direction of the V.A.L.F. and knowing from their General Alarm Bearing signal they had seen it, forbore to investigate.

"There seems little doubt from subsequent analysis that this must have been the remainder of the Italian fleet withdrawing to the north-west. I am of the opinion that the course I selected for withdrawal led the fleet too far to the eastward and that a more northerly course should have been steered."

Barnard has the following to say about the withdrawal order:

"The choice of wording in the actual signal used to convey the Admiral's intentions to disengage unemployed forces to the north-east (i.e. 'All forces not engaged in sinking the enemy retire north-east') was the subject of much discussion in the fleet on return to harbour, and will no doubt be the subject of further armchair critics' remarks in Staff College post mortems in ten years' time [written in 1947]. The writer has no comment of any value to make on this matter, as he was busy peering through night glasses at the time; but on being told the signal had been made, his impression was certainly that it was intended to clear the confused area round the battlefleet, and he and other junior officers thought V.A.L.F. was in contact at the time and would continue shadowing the main body, while D14's destroyers carried out the night attack."

Concerning V.A.L.F.'s actions shortly after seeing the red light, at 10.42 p.m., the staff officer operations, Commander Power, now Admiral Sir Manley Power, K.C.B., C.B.E., D.S.O., has the following comment:

> "The nub of the story, which I only heard years after, was a communication failure and V.A.L.F. was not receiving *Ajax*'s copious radar reports and was not himself aware of the proximity of *Vittorio Veneto*. It is not easy to realise from subsequent readings of signals and reports how completely we in the *Warspite* were convinced from what we had seen and the signals we were receiving, that our destroyers had got right into the Italian fleet just after the battlefleet disengaged to the northeast."

It is interesting to conjecture what would have happened had Cunningham proceeded from Alexandria at higher speed. His speed during the night of the 27th and the early hours of the 28th March was 20 knots and was limited by the condenser trouble in *Warspite* which was later cleared. The speed of 20 knots placed the battlefleet and *Formidable* in a position, at 6.30 a.m., still 150 miles from Pridham-Wippell's rendezvous, a rendezvous which had been decided after receipt of the sighting report shortly after noon on Thursday, 27th March. This rendezvous, 34° 20′ North, 24° 10′ East, bears roughly 114° 360 miles from the sighting position of enemy cruisers by the Sunderland, and therefore could have been reached by the Italian cruisers steering a course of 114° at 20 knots by 6.30 a.m., the time of Pridham-Wippell's rendezvous. In the event, as we have seen, three distinct Italian groups, *Vittorio Veneto* and the two cruiser forces, were in the vicinity at 6.30 a.m. not far distant from Pridham-Wippell himself. It would therefore appear that Cunningham should have had his battlefleet and carrier much further advanced on the mean course of approach. The course from Alexandria is narrowly restricted between 282° by the Cyrenaica coast, and 303° by Crete: a sector of only 21°. There would therefore have been little danger of being too far advanced in the wrong direction by daylight.

The thought comes to mind that *Valiant* and *Formidable* could have been sent on at 24 knots when the battlefleet left Alexandria on the evening of the 27th, with *Warspite* and *Barham* following at best speed, say 20 knots. This would have put them nearly fifty miles farther ahead of the position that was actually reached for the daylight search, resulting in earlier and more accurate reports from *Formidable*'s aircraft, and from them an opportunity to launch earlier torpedo strikes with the object of slowing up the enemy sufficiently for them to be caught by a concentration of the battle-ships before daylight ended. An admiral is, however, loath to divide his force except in emergency or for specific tasks, and, whereas such a risk could have been taken if all the facts that we know now had been known then, it is certain that the shortage of destroyers and the presence of Italian submarines, would prevent most admirals, as it did the Commander-in-Chief, from willingly dividing his force. The loss of a battleship would have been a severe blow: the loss of the *Formidable* would have been crippling.

The master of the fleet says:

> "As regards your particular questions I would imagine that the speed of the Fleet was 20–21 knots during the first night. We did not wish to get further to the westward as we aimed to draw the the Italian battlefleet further to the eastward so that we could engage it with maximum air support. We did not consider send-ing *Valiant* and *Formidable* ahead because our object was to lure the enemy to the eastward."

The Commander-in-Chief sums up in his despatch:

> "The results of the action cannot be viewed with entire satisfaction since the damaged *Vittorio Veneto* was allowed to escape. The failure of the cruisers and destroyers to make contact with her during the night was unlucky and is much to be regretted. Nevertheless, substantial results were achieved in the destruction of the three *Zara* class cruisers. These fast, well-armed and armoured ships had always been a source of anxiety as a threat to our own less well-armed cruisers and I was well content to see them disposed of in this summary fashion. There is little doubt that the rough handling given to the enemy on this occasion served us in good stead during the subsequent evacuation of Greece and Crete. Much of these later operations may be said to have been conducted under the cover of the Battle of Matapan."

Barnard writes a postscript to his comments, which gives an interesting slant on one aspect of the victory.

> "Some months after Matapan a legend gained wide currency in the Mediterranean Fleet, which is probably entirely apocryphal, but may be worth reading to give a clue to the form and also to the healthy rivalry between the Mediterranean and Home Fleets which continued in war the sporting rivalries formerly encountered on peace spring cruises.
>
> "The legend was to the effect that ABC's first list of recommendations for honours and awards for Matapan was microscopic and that it was queried by some unnamed high authority, who was alleged to have pointed out that the Home Fleet had occupied several columns of the London Gazette for sinking the *Bismarck* and 'was ABC sure he hadn't forgotten anyone?' To which the reply, according to bar gossip in Alexandria, was supposed to have been 'Certainly not, no officer did other than his bare duty. If they had done any less I would have had them dismissed for incompetence or shot for negligence.' So perhaps there are some officers alive today, whom His Majesty the King was ultimately pleased to honour for this action, who keep to themselves the salutary thought that their Commander-in-Chief might very justifiably have had them shot for negligence if they had acted other than as they did.
>
> "As regards his own high honour for the general conduct of operations in the Eastern Mediterranean, the same sources report that, when ABC was informed that His Majesty was proposing to award him the G.C.B., he said with all sincerity: 'I wish he'd send me three squadrons of Hurricanes.'"

It was not until two years later that North Africa was cleared of the enemy by the British Eighth Army and that all danger to the sea route through the Eastern Mediterranean was removed. During these two years we suffered grievous losses in warships and merchant ships, through enemy submarine and air attacks, but never did we lose control of the great sea route to the East, and never did we suffer sustained interference from surface forces, though the moment was often critical. The German hope that Italian units would seize the "favourable moment" to interfere with British shipping and interrupt the transport of inadequately protected British troops was shattered. Cunningham's night action off Cape Matapan virtually put the great gateway to the East out of bounds to the Italian Fleet for the rest of the war.

17

Postscript

ON 1ST APRIL a special thanksgiving service for the victory off
Cape Matapan was held on board all ships of the Mediterranean
Fleet at Alexandria. Let us mark well the sailors' prayer which was
said on that occasion: a prayer for use in the Royal Navy every
day. The only change that takes place in this lovely prayer, as
the years and centuries pass, is in the name of our gracious
Sovereign. The desire for peace and quietness in our Island, and
in the dominions under our gracious Sovereign, remains. Let us
never forget those Fleets, without whose continued operation on
the seas upon their lawful occasions such peace and quietness
could be denied us.

Prayer to be used in the Royal Navy every day

O Eternal Lord God, who alone spreadest out the heavens
and rulest the raging of the sea; who hast compassed the waters
with bounds until day and night come to an end; be pleased to
receive into thy Almighty and most gracious protection the
persons of us thy Servants, and the Fleet in which we serve.
Preserve us from the dangers of the sea, and from the violence
of the enemy: that we may be a safeguard unto our most
gracious Sovereign lady, Queen Elizabeth, and her dominions,
and a security for such as pass on the seas upon their lawful
occasions: that the inhabitants of our Island may in peace and
quietness serve thee our God; and that we may return in safety
to enjoy the blessings of the land, with the fruits of our labours,
and with a thankful remembrance of thy mercies to praise and
glorify thy Holy Name: through Jesus Christ our Lord.

Amen.

Appendixes
and
Index

Appendix I

British Warships at the Battle of Matapan

(*a*) BATTLESHIPS:

Warspite   30,600 tons, 24 knots, eight 15-inch, eight 6-inch.
Flagship of Commander-in-Chief, Mediterranean.
Admiral Sir Andrew Cunningham, K.C.B., D.S.O.
Captain D. B. Fisher, C.B.E.

Barham   31,000 tons, 23 knots, eight 15-inch, twelve 6-inch.
Flagship of Rear-Admiral 1st Battle Squadron.
Rear-Admiral H. B. Rawlings, O.B.E.
Captain G. C. Cooke.

Valiant   31,520 tons, 24 knots, eight 15-inch, twenty 4·5-inch.
Captain C. E. Morgan, D.S.O.

(*b*) AIRCRAFT CARRIER:

Formidable   23,000 tons, 30·5 knots, sixteen 4·5-inch.
Flagship Rear Admiral (Air).
Rear-Admiral D. W. Boyd, C.B.E., D.S.C.
Captain A. W. La T. Bisset.

(*c*) AIRCRAFT SQUADRONS:

803 (*Formidable*) Lieutenant K. M. Bruen.
826 (*Formidable*) Lieutenant-Commander W. H. G. Saunt.
829 (*Formidable*) Lieutenant-Commander J. Dalyell-Stead.
815 (Maleme) Lieutenant F. M. A. Torrens-Spence.

(*d*) CRUISERS:

Orion   7,215 tons, 32·5 knots, eight 6-inch.
Flagship of Vice-Admiral Light Forces.
Vice-Admiral H. D. Pridham-Wippell C.B., C.V.O.
Captain G. R. B. Back

Ajax   6,985 tons, 32·5 knots, eight 6-inch.
Captain E. D. B. McCarthy.

Perth   7,165 tons, 32·5 knots, eight 6-inch.
Captain Sir P. W. Bowyer-Smyth, Bart.

| Gloucester | 9,600 tons, 32·3 knots, twelve 6-inch. |
| | Captain H. A. Rowley. |

(*e*) DESTROYERS

14th Destroyer Flotilla

Jervis	1,760 tons, 36 knots, six 4·7-inch, one 4-inch H.A.
	Captain P. J. Mack, D.S.O.
Janus	1,760 tons, 36 knots, six 4·7 inch, one 4-inch H.A.
	Lieutenant L. R. P. Lawford.
Mohawk	1,870 tons, 36·5 knots, eight 4·7-inch.
	Commander J. W. M. Eaton
Nubian	1,870 tons, 36·5 knots, eight 4·7-inch.
	Commander R. W. Ravenhill.

10th Destroyer Flotilla

Stuart	1,530 tons, 36·5 knots, five 4·7-inch, one 3-inch H.A.
	Captain H. M. L. Waller, D.S.O., R.A.N.
Greyhound	1,335 tons, 36 knots, four 4·7-inch, one 3-inch H.A.
	Commander W. R. Marshall-A'Deane, D.S.C.
Griffin	1,335 tons, 36 knots, four 4·7-inch, one 3-inch H.A.
	Lieutenant-Commander J. Lee-Barber, D.S.O.

2nd Destroyer Flotilla

Ilex	1,370 tons, 36 knots, four 4·7-inch.
	Captain H. St. L. Nicholson, D.S.O.
Hasty	1,340 tons, 36 knots, four 4·7-inch.
	Lieutenant-Commander L. R. K. Tyrwhitt.
Hereward	1,340 tons, 36 knots, four 4·7-inch.
	Lieutenant T. F. P. U. Page.
Havock	1,340 tons, 36 knots, four 4·7-inch.
	Lieutenant G. R. G. Watkins.
Hotspur	1,340 tons, 36 knots, four 4·7-inch, one 3-inch H.A.
	Lieutenant-Commander C. P. F. Brown, D.S.C.

Appendix II

Italian Warships at the Battle of Matapan

(*a*) BATTLESHIP:

Vittorio Veneto   35,000 tons, 30·5 knots, nine 15-inch, twelve 6-inch.
Flagship of Commander-in-Chief.
Admiral A. Iachino.

(*b*) CRUISERS:

3rd Division

Trieste	10,000 tons, 35 knots, eight 8-inch.
	Flagship of Vice-Admiral L. Sansonetti.
Trento	10,000 tons, 35 knots, eight 8-inch.
Bolzano	10,000 tons, 36 knots, eight 8-inch.

1st Division

(Sunk) Zara	10,000 tons, 32 knots, eight 8-inch.
	Flagship of Vice-Admiral C. Cattaneo.
	Captain L. Cossi.
(Sunk) Fiume	10,000 tons, 32 knots, eight 8-inch.
	Captain G. Giorgis.
(Sunk) Pola	10,000 tons, 32 knots, eight 8-inch.
	Captain M. de Pisa.

8th Division

Abruzzi	7,874 tons, 35 knots, ten 6-inch.
	Flagship of Vice-Admiral A. Legnani.
Garibaldi	7,874 tons, 35 knots, ten 6-inch.

(*c*) DESTROYERS

6th Destroyer Flotilla

Da Recco	1,628 tons, 39 knots, six 4·7-inch.
Pessagno	1,628 tons, 39 knots, six 4·7-inch.

9th Destroyer Flotilla

Gioberti	1,568 tons, 39 knots, four 4·7-inch.
(Sunk) Alfieri	1,568 tons, 39 knots, four 4·7-inch.
Oriani	1,568 tons, 39 knots, four 4·7-inch.
(Sunk) Carducci	1,568 tons, 39 knots, four 4·7-inch.

10th Destroyer Flotilla

Maestrale	1,449 tons, 39 knots, four 4·7-inch.
Libeccio	1,449 tons, 39 knots, four 4·7-inch.
Scirocco	1,449 tons, 39 knots, four 4·7-inch.
Gregale	1,449 tons, 39 knots, four 4·7-inch.

12th Destroyer Flotilla

Corazziere	1,620 tons, 39 knots, five 4·7-inch.
Carabiniere	1,620 tons, 39 knots, five 4·7-inch.
Ascari	1,620 tons, 39 knots, five 4·7-inch.

13th Destroyer Flotilla

Granatiere	1,620 tons, 39 knots, five 4·7-inch.
Fuciliere	1,620 tons, 39 knots, five 4·7-inch.
Bersagliere	1,620 tons, 39 knots, five 4·7-inch.
Alpino	1,620 tons, 39 knots, five 4·7-inch.

Appendix III

Table of Air Attacks on Italian Ships during 28th March, 1941, compiled from British and Italian Reports

Time	Position	Aircraft	Squadron	Target	Weapon	Result
1120 to 1130	34°06′N. 23°58′E.	6 Albacores 2 Fulmars	F.A.A. 826 F.A.A. 803	*Veneto*	Tor- pedoes	No hits
1205	34°04′N. 23°22′E.	3 Swordfish	F.A.A. 815	3rd Division	Tor- pedoes	No hits
1420	34°38′N. 22°30′E.	3 Blenheims	R.A.F. 84	*Veneto*	Bombs	No hits
1450	34°42′N. 22°15′E.	6 Blenheims	R.A.F. 113	*Veneto*	Bombs	No hits
1510 to 1525	34°50′N. 22°00′E.	3 Albacores 2 Swordfish 2 Fulmars	F.A.A. 829 F.A.A. 829 F.A.A. 803	*Veneto*	Tor- pedoes	One hit on *Veneto*
1515 to 1645	Between 35°30′N. 21°22′E. and 35°43′N. 20°58′E.	6 Blenheims 5 Blenheims	R.A.F. 113 R.A.F. 84	1st Division 1st Division	Bombs Bombs	Near misses on *Zara* and *Garibaldi*
1520 to 1700	34°49′N. 21°50′E. 35°03′N. 21°21′E.	4 Blenheims 6 Blenheims	R.A.F. 84 R.A.F. 211	3rd Division 3rd Division	Bombs Bombs	Near misses on *Trento* and *Bolzano*
1930 to 1950	35°15′N. 20°58′E.	6 Albacores 2 Swordfish 2 Swordfish	F.A.A. 826 F.A.A. 829 F.A.A. 815	1st Division	Tor- pedoes	One hit on *Pola*

Appendix IV

Formidable's Log of Flying Operations—28th March, 1941

Time	Operation	Duty	Remarks
0550–0558	Fly off	5 T.S.R.,* search 1 T.S.R., A/S patrol 2 fighters, patrol	M.L.A. 310°/16 knots into wind 050°
0749	Boost	1 fighter, patrol	Second fighter could not be fitted to A.T.O.
0802–0808	Fly off	1 fighter, patrol 1 T.S.R., A/S patrol	M.L.A. 310°/16 knots into wind 040°
	Land on	2 fighters, patrol 1 T.S.R., patrol	,,
0952–1004	Fly off	2 fighters, escort 6 T.S.R., strike 1 T.S.R., duty J	M.L.A. 300°/22 knots into wind 040°
	Land on	2 fighters, patrol 1 T.S.R., search 1 T.S.R., A/S patrol	
1045–1050	Fly off	2 fighters, patrol	M.L.A. 300°/22 knots
	Land on	2 T.S.R., search	into wind 040°
1131–1133	Land on	1 T.S.R., search	Carrier turned into wind independently
1222–1243	Fly off	5 T.S.R., strike 1 T.S.R., duty K 2 fighters, escort	Carrier turned into wind independently
	Land on	6 T.S.R., strike 2 fighters, escort 2 fighters, patrol 1 Walrus (*Gloucester*)	
1312–1315	Fly off	4 fighters, patrol	
1355	Boost	2 fighters, patrol	

* T.S.R. = Torpedo-Spotting-Reconnaissance aircraft (Albacore or Swordfish)
A/S = Anti-Submarine

Time	Operation	Duty	Remarks
1357–1404	Fly off	3 T.S.R., search 1 Walrus (*Gloucester*)	From this point on, flying operations carried out with B.F. by small alterations of course, carrier remaining under cover of B.F. screen.
	Land on	1 T.S.R., duty J	
1450–1455	Fly off	1 T.S.R., search	Additional aircraft to fill gaps.
1516–1520	Fly off	2 fighters, patrol	
	Land on	4 fighters, patrol	
1554–1605	Land on	4 T.S.R., strike 1 T.S.R., search 1 T.S.R., duty K 2 fighters, patrol 2 fighters, escort	
1648–1700	Fly off	4 fighters, patrol	
	Land on	1 fighter (engine trouble) 1 T.S.R., search	
1730–1740	Fly off	8 T.S.R., dusk strike	To land ashore
	Land on	2 fighters, patrol	
1745–1746	Land on	1 T.S.R., search	
1751–1755	Boost	3 fighters, patrol	
1840–1841	Fly off	1 T.S.R., night shadowing	To land ashore
1853–1855	Land on	3 fighters, patrol	
1905–1910	Land on	3 fighters, patrol	
1942–1943	Land on	1 T.S.R., search and shadowing	
1943			Flying completed

Appendix V

Crews of Formidable's Torpedo Strike Aircraft

No.	Pilot	Observer	Telegraphist-Air Gunner
FORENOON STRIKE			
4A	Lt.-Cdr. Saunt	Lt. Hopkins	—
4F	Lt. Ellis	Lt. Haworth	—
4C	Sub.-Lt. Bradshaw	Sub.-Lt. Drummond	—
4K	Lt. Abrams	Lt. Smith Shand	—
4P	Sub.-Lt. Tuke	Sub.-Lt. Mallett	—
5A	Sub.-Lt. Williams	Mid. Davis	A/L. Booth
AFTERNOON STRIKE			
5G	Lt.-Cdr. Dalyell-Stead	Lt. Cooke	P.O. Blenkhorn
5F	Lt. Whitworth	Sub.-Lt. Ellis	A/L. Morris
5H	Sub.-Lt. Bibby	Sub.-Lt. Parrish	A/L. Hogg
*5K	Lt. Osborn	Lt. Pain	P.O. Montague
*4B	Lt. Smith	Unrecorded	Unrecorded
DUSK STRIKE			
4A	Lt.-Cdr. Saunt	Lt. Hopkins	—
4K	Lt. Abrams	Lt. Smith Shand	—
4P	Sub.-Lt. Tuke	Sub.-Lt. Wilson	—
*4H	Sub.-Lt. Thorpe	Lt. Rushworth Lund	A. Japp
5A	Sub.-Lt. Williams	Mid. Davis	A/L. Booth
5F	Lt. Whitworth	Sub.-Lt. Ellis	A/L. Morris
5H	Sub.-Lt. Bibby	Sub.-Lt. Parrish	A/L. Hogg
*5K	Lt. Osborn	Lt. Pain	P.O. Montague

Supplemented by two Swordfish from 815 Squadron at Maleme

	*Lt. Torrens-Spence	Unrecorded	Unrecorded
	*Sub.-Lt. Kiggell	Unrecorded	Unrecorded

* Signifies that the aircraft was a Swordfish; the remainder were all Albacores.

Index

The numerals in **heavy type** refer to the *figure numbers* of the illustrations.

179